The History of Presidential Assassination in America

SB Jeffrey

The role of the book within our culture is changing. The change is brought on by new ways to acquire & use content, the rapid dissemination of information and real-time peer collaboration on a global scale. Despite these changes one thing is clear--"the book" in it's traditional form continues to play an important role in learning and communication. The book you are holding in your hands utilizes the unique characteristics of the Internet -- relying on web infrastructure and collaborative tools to share and use resources in keeping with the characteristics of the medium (user-created, defying control, etc.)--while maintaining all the convenience and utility of a real book.

Contents

Articles

The History of Political Assassination — **1**
- Assassination — 1
- History of assassination — 16

The First Attempt on A President — **24**
- Richard Lawrence (failed assassin) — 24

The Death of A President — **26**
- John Wilkes Booth — 26

Two Ohio Presidents are Assassinated — **49**
- Charles J. Guiteau — 49
- Leon Czolgosz — 55

The Kennedy Brothers — **62**
- Lee Harvey Oswald — 62
- John F. Kennedy assassination conspiracy theories — 78
- Sirhan Sirhan — 99
- Assassination of Robert F. Kennedy — 105

Modern Failed Attempts — **113**
- Lynette Fromme — 113
- Sara Jane Moore — 118
- John Hinckley, Jr. — 121

References

| Article Sources and Contributors | 126 |
| Image Sources, Licenses and Contributors | 127 |

The History of Political Assassination

Assassination

"Assassin" and "Assassins" redirect here. For other uses, see Assassin (disambiguation).

Homicide
Murder
Note: Varies by jurisdiction
Assassination · Child murder Consensual homicide Contract killing · Felony murder rule Honor killing · Human sacrifice Lust murder · Lynching Mass murder · Murder–suicide Proxy murder · Lonely hearts killer Serial killer · Spree killer Torture murder · Feticide Double murder · Misdemeanor murder Crime of passion · Internet homicide Depraved-heart murder
Manslaughter
in English law Negligent homicide Vehicular homicide
Non-criminal homicide
Note: Varies by jurisdiction

Justifiable homicide
Capital punishment
Human sacrifice
Feticide
Medicide
By victim or victims
Suicide
Family
Familicide · Avunculicide
Prolicide
(Filicide • Infanticide • Neonaticide)
Fratricide / Sororicide
Mariticide / Uxoricide
Parricide
(Matricide • Patricide)
Other
Amicicide
Genocide / Democide
Gendercide
Omnicide
Regicide / Tyrannicide
Pseudocide
Deicide

An **assassination** is the murder of a prominent or public figure, usually by surprise attack and for political purposes.

Assassinations may be prompted by religious, ideological, political, or military reasons. Additionally, assassins may be motivated by financial gain, revenge, or personal public recognition.

Assassination may also refer to the government-sanctioned killing of opponents or to targeted attacks on high-profile enemy combatants.

Etymology

Main article: Hashshashin

The word *assassin* is derived from the word *Hashshashin* (Arabic: حَشَّاشين, also Hashishin, Hashashiyyin or Assassins) and share its etymological roots with *hashish* (pronounced /hæˈʃiːʃ/ or English pronunciation: /ˈhæʃiːʃ/) (from Arabic: حشيش *ḥashīsh*), referred to the Nizari branch of the Ismāʿīlī Shia under the instruction of Hassan aṣ-Ṣabbaḥ during the Middle Ages. They were active in the fort of

Alamut in Iran from the eighth to the fourteenth centuries. They also controlled castle of Masyaf in Syria. This group killed members of the elites of both Muslim Abbasid, Seljuq and Christian Crusaders élite for political and religious reasons. They were feared among the crusaders, the Muslims and the Knights Templar for their power and tactics.

The Hashshashin were eradicated by the Mongol Empire and the well documented invasion of Khwarizm. They probably dispatched their assassins to kill Mongke Khan. Thus a decree was handed over to the Mongol commander Kitbuqa who began to assault several Hashshashin fortresses in 1253 before Hulegu advance in 1256. The Mongol besieged Alamut on December 15, 1256. The Hashshashin recaptured and held Alamut for a few months in 1275 but they were crushed and their political power was lost forever. Thus ended the reign of one of the most feared sects in the whole world.

Although commonly believed that assassins were under the influence of hashish during their killings or during their indoctrination, there is continued debate within the historical community whether these claims have any merit, as direct evidence from any contemporary source, Nizari or otherwise, is non-existent. Marco Polo and subsequent European visitors to the area received from rivals of the Nizarai, what were to these opponents, derogatory names for the Nizarai Ismaili, and significantly embroidered stories about them. Polo, Henry II, Count of Champagne, William Marsden, an envoy of Frederick Barbarossa, William, Archbishop of Tyre and others following, popularized the names and stories in Europe, oblivious to their origin in factional propaganda.

The earliest known literary use of the word *assassination* is in *Macbeth* by William Shakespeare (1605).

Use in history

Main article: History of assassination

Ancient to medieval times

Assassination is one of the oldest tools of power politics, dating back at least as far as recorded history. Perhaps the earliest recorded instance is the murder of the Moabite King, Eglon by Ehud around 1337 BC, described by The Book of Judges. Philip II of Macedon, the father of Alexander the Great, and Julius Caesar are famous victims. Emperors of Rome often met their end in this way, as did many of the Shia Imams. The practice was also well known in ancient China. An example of this is Jing Ke's failed assassination of Qin Shi Huang. The ancient Indian military adviser Chanakya wrote about assassinations in detail in his political treatise *Arthashastra*. On April 28, 1192, Conrad of Montferrat was assassinated by two hashshashin.

The apocryphal Old Testament story of Judith illustrates how a woman frees the Israelites by tricking and assassinating Holofernes, a war-lord of the rival Assyrians with whom the Israelites were at war.

In the Middle Ages, regicide was rare in Western Europe, but it was a recurring theme in the Eastern Roman Empire. Blinding and strangling in the bathtub were the most commonly used procedures. With the Renaissance, tyrannicide—or assassination for personal or political reasons—became more common again in Western Europe. The reigns of the French kings Henry III and Henry IV, and William the Silent of the Netherlands ended with assassination.

In modern history

As the world moved into the modern day, the killing of important people began to become more than a tool in power struggles between rulers themselves and was also used for political symbolism, such as in the propaganda of the deed. In Russia alone, four emperors were assassinated within less than two hundred years: Ivan VI, Peter III, Paul I, and Alexander II.

In the United States, four presidents, Abraham Lincoln, James Garfield, William McKinley, and John F. Kennedy died at the hands of assassins. There have been at least 20 known attempts on U.S. presidents' lives.

Assassination of Abraham Lincoln, artist's depiction from 1865. Assassin John Wilkes Booth on the right.

In Europe the assassination of Archduke Franz Ferdinand by Serbian nationalist insurgents (The Black Hand) is blamed for igniting World War I after a succession of minor conflicts, while belligerents on both sides in World War II used operatives specifically trained for assassination. Reinhard Heydrich was killed by Czech partisan killers, and knowledge from decoded transmissions allowed the U.S. to carry out a targeted attack, killing Japanese Admiral Isoroku Yamamoto while he was travelling by plane. The Polish Home Army conducted a regular campaign of assassinations against top Nazi German officials in occupied Poland. Adolf Hitler, meanwhile, was almost killed by his own officers, and survived various attempts by other persons and organizations (such as Operation Foxley, though this plan was never put into practice).

During the 1930s and 1940s Stalin's NKVD carried out numerous assassinations outside of its borders, such as the killings of OUN leader Yevhen Konovalets, Ignacy Porecki-Reiss, Fourth International secretary Rudolf Klement, Leon Trotsky and the POUM leadership in Catalonia.

India's "Father of the Nation," Mohandas K. Gandhi, was shot to death on January 30, 1948, by Nathuram Godse.

Cold War and beyond

See also: Cold War and War on Terrorism

During the Cold War, there was a dramatic new increase in the number of political assassinations, likely due to the ideological polarization of most of the First and Second worlds, whose adherents were often more than willing to both justify and finance such killings.[*citation needed*]

Liaquat Ali Khan, the first Prime Minister of Pakistan, was assassinated by Saad Akbar, a lone assassin, in 1951. Conspiracy theorists believe his conflict with certain members of the Pakistani military (Rawalpindi conspiracy) or suppression of Communists and antagonism towards the Soviet Union, were potential reasons for his assassination.

The U.S. Senate Select Committee chaired by Senator Frank Church (the Church Committee) reported in 1975 that it had found "concrete evidence of at least eight plots involving the CIA to assassinate Fidel Castro from 1960 to 1965."

Most major powers were not long in repudiating Cold War assassination tactics, though many allege that this was merely a smokescreen for political benefit and that covert and illegal training of assassins continues today, with Russia, Israel, USA, Argentina, Paraguay, Chile and other nations accused of still regularly engaging in such operations. In 1986, U.S. President Ronald Reagan (who survived an assassination attempt himself) ordered the Operation El Dorado Canyon air raid on Libya in which one of the primary targets was the home residence of Libyan ruler Muammar Gaddafi. Gaddafi escaped unharmed; however, his adopted daughter Hanna was one of the civilian casualties. In the Philippines, the assassination of Benigno Aquino, Jr. triggered the eventual downfall of the 20-year autocratic rule of President Ferdinand Marcos. Aquino, a former Senator and a leading figure of the political opposition, was assassinated in 1983 at the Manila International Airport (now the Ninoy Aquino International Airport) upon returning home from exile. His death thrust his widow, Corazon Aquino, into the limelight and, ultimately, the presidency following the peaceful 1986 EDSA Revolution.

After the Iranian Revolution of 1979, the new Islamic government of Iran began an international campaign of assassination that lasted into the 1990s. At least 162 killings in 19 different countries have been linked to the senior leadership of the Islamic Republic of Iran. This campaign came to an end after the Mykonos restaurant assassinations, because a German court publicly implicated senior members of the government and issued arrest warrants for Ali Fallahian, the head of the Iranian Intelligence. Evidence indicates that Fallahian's personal involvement and individual responsibility for the murders were far more pervasive than his current indictment record represents.

On August 17, 1988 President of Pakistan Gen. M. Zia ul Haq died along with his staff and the American Ambassador to Pakistan when his C-130 transport plane exploded in mid-air after taking off from Bahawalpur because of an on-board bomb. The CIA, KGB and Indian secret service RAW all have been implicated by various conspiracy theorists.Wikipedia:Avoid weasel words

Various governments around the world, such as Saddam Hussein's, have also used assassination to remove individual opponents, or to terrorize troublesome population groups.[citation needed] In return, in post-Saddam Iraq, the Shiite-dominated government has used death squads to perform countless extrajudicial executions of radical Sunni Iraqis, with some alleging that the death squads were trained by the U.S.

In India, Prime Ministers Indira Gandhi and Rajiv Gandhi (neither of whom were related to Mohandas Gandhi, who was assassinated in 1948), were assassinated in 1984 and 1991. The assassinations were linked to separatist movements in Punjab and northern Sri Lanka, respectively.

In Israel, Prime Minister Yitzhak Rabin was assassinated on November 4, 1995. Yigal Amir confessed and was convicted of the crime. Many questions were subsequently raised about the actual cause of and rationale for his death.

Israeli tourists minister Rehavam Ze'evi was assassinated on October 17, 2001 by Hamdi Quran and three other members of the Popular Front for the Liberation of Palestine (PFLP). The PFLP stated that the assassination was in retaliation for the August 27, 2001 assassination of Abu Ali Mustafa, the Secretary General of the PFLP, by the Israeli Air Force under its policy of targeted killings.

In Lebanon, the assassination of former Prime Minister Rafik Hariri on February 14, 2005, prompted an investigation by the United Nations. The suggestions in the resulting Mehlis report, that there was Syrian involvement, prompted the Cedar Revolution, which drove Syrian troops out of Lebanon.

In Pakistan, former prime minister and opposition leader Benazir Bhutto was assassinated in 2007, while in the process of running for re-election. Bhutto's assassination drew unanimous condemnation from the international community.

In Guinea Bissau, President João Bernardo Vieira was assassinated in the early hours of Monday March 2, 2009 in the capital, Bissau. Unlike typical assassinations his death was not swift; first surviving an explosion at the Presidential Villa before being shot and wounded and finally butchered with machetes. His assassination was carried out by renegade soldiers who were apparently revenging the prior assassination of General Tagme Na Waie, the Chief of Staff of the Armed Forces of Guinea Bissau, who had been killed in a bomb explosion the day before.

In 2002, the George W. Bush Administration prepared a list of "terrorist leaders" the CIA is authorized to assassinate, if capture is impractical and civilian casualties can be kept to an acceptable number. The list includes key al-Qa'ida leaders like Osama bin Laden and his chief deputy, Ayman al-Zawahiri, as well as other principal figures from al-Qa'ida and affiliated groups. This list is called the "high value target list". The US president is not legally required to approve each name added to the list, nor is the CIA required to obtain presidential approval for specific attacks, although the president is kept well informed about operations.

President Obama's CIA Director Leon Panetta stated that Special Activities Division efforts in Pakistan have been "the most effective weapon" against senior al-Qa'ida leadership.

On July 14, 2009, several newspapers reported that CIA director Leon Panetta was briefed on a CIA program that had not been briefed to the oversight committees in Congress. Panetta cancelled the initiative and reported it to Congress and the President. The program consisted of teams of Special Activities Division paramilitary officers organized to execute targeted assassination operations against al-Qa'ida operatives around the world in any country. According to the Los Angeles Times, DCIA Panetta "has not ruled out reviving the program". There is some question as to whether former Vice President Richard Cheney instructed the CIA not to inform Congress. Per senior intelligence officers, this program was an attempt to avoid the civilian casualties that can occur during Predator drone strikes using Hellfire missiles.

On July 22, 2009, National Public Radio reported that U.S. officials believe Saad bin Laden, a son of Osama bin Laden, was assassinated by a CIA strike in Pakistan. Saad bin Laden spent years under house arrest in Iran before traveling last year to Pakistan, according to former National Intelligence Director Mike McConnell. It is believed he was killed sometime in 2009. A senior U.S. counterterrorism said U.S. intelligence agencies are "80 to 85 percent" certain that Saad bin Laden is dead.

Further motivations

As military doctrine

See also: Manhunt (military)

Assassination for military purposes has long been espoused – Sun Tzu, writing around 500 BC, argued in favor of using assassination in his book *The Art of War*. Nearly 2000 years later Machiavelli also argued assassination could be useful in his book *The Prince*.[citation needed] In medieval times, an army and even a nation might be based upon and around a particularly strong, canny or charismatic leader, whose loss could paralyze the ability of both to make war. However, in modern warfare a soldier's mindset is generally considered to surround ideals far more than specific leaders, while command structures are more flexible in replacing officer losses. While the death of a popular or successful leader often has a detrimental effect on morale, the organizational system and the belief in a specific cause is usually strong enough to enable continued warfare.

There is also the risk that the target could be replaced by an even more competent leader or such a killing (or a failed attempt) will "martyr" a leader and support his cause (by showing the moral ruthlessness of the assassins). Faced with particularly brilliant leaders, this possibility has in various instances been risked, such as in the attempts to kill the Athenian Alcibiades during the Peloponnesian War. A number of additional examples from World War II show how assassination was used as a military tool at both tactical and strategic levels:

- The American interception of Admiral Isoroku Yamamoto's plane during World War II, after his travel route had been decrypted.

- The American perception that Skorzeny's commandos were planning to assassinate Eisenhower during the Battle of the Bulge played havoc with Eisenhower's personal plans for some time, though it did not affect the battle itself. Skorzeny later denied in an interview with *The New York Times*[citation needed] that he had ever intended to assassinate Eisenhower during Operation Greif and he said that he could prove it.
- Operation Gaff was a planned British commando raid to capture or kill the German Field Marshal Erwin Rommel (also known as "The Desert Fox").

Use of assassination has continued in more recent conflicts:

- During the Vietnam War, partly in response to Viet Cong assassinations of government leaders, the USA engaged in the Phoenix Program to assassinate Viet Cong leaders and sympathizers, and killed between 6,000 and 41,000 persons, with official 'targets' of 1,800 per month.
- From 1991 till 2006, Russia targeted the top commanders of the separatist groups they were fighting in Chechnya, killing several of them (including Aslan Maskhadov and Shamil Basayev)
- In the Global War on Terrorism, American special operations forces and intelligence agencies employed manhunting operations against key opponents and Al Qaeda terrorist leaders.

As tool of insurgents

Insurgent groups have often employed assassination as a tool to further their causes. Assassinations provide several functions for such groups, namely the removal of specific enemies and as propaganda tools to focus the attention of media and politics on their cause.

The Irish Republican Army guerrillas of 1919–1921 assassinated many RIC Police Intelligence officers during the Irish War of Independence. Michael Collins set up a special unit – the Squad – for this purpose, which had the effect of intimidating many policemen into resigning from the force. The Squad was headed by the infamous Bevis Pole. The Squad's activities peaked with the assassination of 14 British agents in Dublin on Bloody Sunday in 1920.

This tactic was used again by the Provisional IRA during the Troubles in Northern Ireland (1969–present). Assassination of RUC officers and politicians was one of a number of methods used in the Provisional IRA campaign 1969-1997. The IRA also attempted to assassinate British Prime Minister Margaret Thatcher by bombing the Conservative Party Conference in a Brighton hotel. Loyalist paramilitaries retaliated by killing Catholics at random and assassinating Irish nationalist politicians.

Basque terrorists ETA in Spain have assassinated many security and political figures since the late 1960s, notably Luis Carrero Blanco in 1973. Since the early 1990s, they have also targeted academics, journalists and local politicians who publicly disagreed with them, meaning that many needed armed police bodyguards.

The Red Brigades in Italy carried out assassinations of political figures, as to a lesser extent, did the Red Army Faction in Germany in the 1970s and 1980s.

Middle Eastern groups, such as the PLO and Hezbollah, have all engaged in assassinations, though the higher intensity of armed conflict in the region compared to western Europe means that many of their actions are either better characterized as guerrilla operations or as random attacks – especially the technique of suicide bombs.

In the Vietnam War, assassinations were routinely carried out by communist insurgents against government officials and individual civilians deemed to offend or rival the revolutionary movement. Such attacks, along with widespread military activity by insurgent bands, almost brought the Diem regime to collapse before the US intervention.

Targeted killing

Main article: Targeted killing

Author and Red Cross legal adviser Nils Melzer defines targeted killing as "the use of lethal force attributable to a subject of international law with the intent, premeditation and deliberation to kill individually selected persons who are not in the physical custody of those targeting them". The concept and term "targeted killing" has been accepted as part of legal doctrine by some governments and media organizations.[citation needed]

The use of assassinations for political or military reasons by sovereign states is an extremely contentious subject, with opinions ranging from people considering it a legitimate form of defense, especially against non-state actors like terror groups, to people calling targeted killings state terrorism itself.[citation needed] In addition, challenges arise when one considers targeted killing in the context of both international humanitarian law and international human rights law. Both those for and against targeted killings are also often faced with accusations of being clearly partisan to one side of the particular struggle discussed.

- **Pro**: Various groups and individuals have supported targeted killings, such as those undertaken by Israel against groups it considers terrorist, claiming that the killing of people such as Sheikh Ahmed Yassin is justified because people like him provide "both religious and political cover" (for opposed groups to operate), and that the fact that they may not have been physically involved in committing such crimes does not reduce their role or responsibility. Arguing that the killings may produce leadership vacuums and disorganise their organisations. They also oppose the use of the term assassination, as it denotes murder, where targeting such leaders is seen as self-defence, and thus killing, but not a crime. They argue that there is evidence that target killing has been salutary in reducing the *effectiveness* of terrorist attacks. After Israel adopted a policy of targeted killings, deaths resulting from terrorist attacks by Hamas plunged from a high of 75 in 2001, to 21 in 2005. Some argue that even if the killing has little effect on the number and severity of terrorist attacks, targeted killing is appropriate for 'retribution and revenge'. Others make a case that targeted killing adheres to the international law concepts of proportionality and distinction, as the minimum level of force needed to carry out legitimate self-defense. When faced with alternatives of military invasion, carpet bombing, or artillery barrage, targeted killing, while regrettable, is deemed preferable.[citation needed]

- The United States views targeted killing during an armed conflict as the lawful right to use force "consistent with its inherent right to self-defense" under international law in response to the 9/11 attacks. Under domestic law, American targeted killings against 9/11-related entities is authorized by the Authorization for Use of Military Force Against Terrorists.
- On December 14, 2006, the Israeli Supreme Court ruled that targeted killing as carried out by the Israel Defense Forces and Mossad is a legitimate form of self-defense against terrorists, and outlined several conditions for its use.

- **Con**: Criticism of targeted killings focuses on a number of aspects, from being claimed to be against international law, to being asserted to be destabilising to local situations and thus causing more violence, an opinion held by intermediary Álvaro de Soto, former UN Middle East peace envoy. Criticism often also focuses on the killing of innocent victims in heavy-handed failed targeted killings, in which civilians may be killed.
  - Specific legal concerns center on historical uncertainties related to the limits to state sovereignty, the right to use force, and the best means to safeguard civilians – both in protecting them from harm from external threats and in limiting possible incidental harm when combating those external threats. Legal questions include:
    - What constitutes an 'imminent threat' under international law?
    - What constitutes an 'armed conflict' under international law?
    - Does the legal justification change if an unmanned aerial vehicle remote pilot is a military contractor? A civilian?
    - Does the legal justification change if the remote pilot is under the effective control of a civilian?
    - If other States are silent on drone flyovers, does that acquiescence convey political acceptance? Legal acceptance?
    - Is it lawful to assist, or collaborate with, other States to conduct drone attacks when the assisting State is not threatened?
    - Who determines whether a State is unwilling or unable to suppress a threat within its territory?
    - Who determines whether the target is 'legitimate'?
    - Can drones be used in a case of pre-emptive self-defense? If so, when? Does 'intent' by an enemy group constitute legal grounds for a pre-emptive strike?

Targeted killings are also sometimes called "extrajudicial punishment", as some states require some form of judicial trial in absentia before such an undertaking.

Psychology

A major study about assassination attempts in the US in the second half of the 20th century came to the conclusion that most prospective assassins spend copious amounts of time planning and preparing for their attempts. Assassinations are thus rarely a case of 'impulsive' action.

However, about 25% of the actual attackers were found to be delusional, a figure that rose to 60% with 'near-lethal approachers' (people apprehended before reaching their target). This incidentally shows that while mental instability plays a role in many modern-age assassinations, the more delusional attackers are less likely to succeed in their attempt. The report also found that around two thirds of the attackers had previously been arrested for (not necessarily related) offenses, that around 44% had a history of serious depression, and that 39% had a history of substance abuse.

Techniques

Ancient methods

It seems likely that the first assassinations would have been direct and simple: stabbing, strangling or bludgeoning. Substantial planning or coordination would rarely have been involved, as tribal groups were too small, and the connection to the leaders too close. As civilization took root, however, leaders began to have greater importance, and become more detached from the groups they ruled. This would have brought planning, subterfuge and weapons into successful assassination plans.[citation needed]

The key technique was likely infiltration, with the actual assassination by stabbing, smothering or strangulation. Poisons also started to be used in many forms. Death cap mushrooms and similar plants became a traditional choice of assassins especially if they could not be perceived as poisonous by taste, and the symptoms of the poisoning did not show until after some time.[citation needed]

In ancient Rome, paid mobs were sometimes used to beat political enemies to death.[citation needed]

Modern methods

With the advent of effective ranged weaponry, and later firearms, the position of an assassination target was more precarious. Bodyguards were no longer enough to hold back determined killers, who no longer needed to directly engage or even subvert the guard to kill the leader in question. Moreover, the engagement of targets at greater distance dramatically increased the chances for an assassin's survival. The first heads of government to be assassinated with a firearm were the Regent Moray of Scotland in 1570, and William the Silent of the Netherlands in 1584.

Gunpowder and other explosives also allowed the use of bombs or even greater concentrations of explosives for deeds requiring a larger touch; for an example, the Gunpowder Plot could have 'assassinated' almost a thousand people had it not been foiled.

Explosives, especially the car bomb, become far more common in modern history, with grenades and remote-triggered land mines also used, especially in the Middle East and Balkans (the initial attempt on Archduke Franz Ferdinand's life was with a grenade). With heavy weapons, the rocket-propelled grenade (RPG) has become a useful tool given the popularity of armored cars (discussed below), while Israeli forces have pioneered the use of aircraft-mounted missiles for assassination, as well as the innovative use of explosive devices.

A sniper with a precision rifle is often used in fictional assassinations. However, there are certain difficulties associated with long-range shooting, including finding a hidden shooting position with a clear line-of-sight, detailed advance knowledge of the intended victim's travel plans, the ability to identify the target at long range, and the ability to score a first-round lethal hit at long range, usually measured in hundreds of meters. A dedicated sniper rifle is also expensive, often costing thousands of dollars because of the high level of precision machining and hand-finishing required to achieve extreme accuracy.

Despite their comparative disadvantages, handguns are more easily concealable, and consequentially much more commonly used than rifles. Of 74 principal incidents evaluated in a major study about assassination attempts in the US in the second half of the 20th century, 51% were undertaken by a handgun, 30% with a rifle or shotgun, while 15% of the attempts used knives and 8% explosives (usage of multiple weapons/methods was reported in 16% of all cases).

In the case of state-sponsored assassination, poisoning can be more easily denied. Georgi Markov, a Bulgarian dissident was assassinated by ricin poisoning. A tiny pellet containing the poison was injected into his leg through a specially designed umbrella. Widespread allegations involving the Bulgarian government and KGB have not led to any legal results. However, it was learned that after fall of the USSR, the KGB had developed an umbrella that could inject ricin pellets into a victim, and two former KGB agents who defected said the agency assisted in the murder. The CIA has allegedly made several attempts to assassinate Fidel Castro, many of the schemes involving poisoning his milkshakes. In the late 1950s, KGB assassin Bohdan Stashynsky killed Ukrainian nationalist leaders Lev Rebet and Stepan Bandera with a spray gun that fired a jet of poison gas from a crushed cyanide ampule, making their deaths look like heart attacks. A 2006 case in the UK concerned the assassination of Alexander Litvinenko who was given a lethal dose of radioactive polonium-210, possibly passed to him in aerosol form sprayed directly onto his food. Litvinenko, a former KGB agent, had been granted asylum in the UK in 2000 after citing persecution in Russia. Shortly before his death he issued a statement accusing then-President of Russia Vladimir Putin of involvement in his assassination. President Putin denies he had any part in Litvinenko's death.

James Bell proposed "Assassination Politics" both as a political idea and as a logical consequence of anonymous cash. Essentially anonymous contributors fund those who can predict the time and manner of a given person's death; the "predictor" is also paid anonymously.

Counter-measures

Early forms

One of the earliest forms of defense against assassins was employing bodyguards. Bodyguards act as a shield for the potential target, keeping lookout for potential attackers (sometimes in advance, for example on a parade route), and literally putting themselves 'in harm's way'—both by simple presence, showing that physical force is available to protect the target, and by shielding the target during any attack. To neutralize an attacker, bodyguards are typically armed as much as legal and practical concerns permit.

This bodyguard function was often executed by the leader's most loyal warriors, and was extremely effective throughout most of early human history, leading assassins to attempt stealthy means, such as poison (which risk was answered by having another person taste the leader's food first).

Another notable measure is the use of a body double, a person who looks like the leader and who pretends to be the leader to draw attention away from the intended target.[citation needed]

Notable examples of bodyguards include the Roman Praetorian Guard or the Ottoman Janissaries--although, in both cases, the protectors sometimes became assassins themselves, exploiting their power to make the head of state a virtual hostage or killing the very leaders they were supposed to protect. The fidelity of individual bodyguards is an important question as well, especially for leaders who oversee states with strong ethnic or religious divisions. Failure to realize such divided loyalties led to the assassination of Indian Prime Minister Indira Gandhi, assassinated by two Sikh bodyguards in 1984.

Modern strategies

With the advent of gunpowder, ranged assassination (via bombs or firearms) became possible. One of the first reactions was to simply increase the guard, creating what at times might seem a small army trailing every leader; another was to begin clearing large areas whenever a leader was present, to the point where entire sections of a city might be shut down.

As the 20th century dawned, the prevalence of assassins and their capabilities skyrocketed, and so did measures to protect against them. For the first time, armored cars or armored limousines were put into service for safer transport, with modern versions rendering them virtually invulnerable to small arms fire and smaller bombs and mines. Bulletproof vests also began to be used, though they were of limited utility, restricting movement and leaving the head unprotected – as such they tended to be worn only during high-profile public events if at all.

Access to famous persons, too, became more and more restricted; potential visitors would be forced through numerous different checks before being granted access to the official in question, and as communication became better and information technology more prevalent, it has become all but impossible for a would-be killer to get close enough to the personage at work or in private life to effect an attempt on his or her life, especially given the common use of metal and bomb detectors. This is, of course, assuming that the assassin does not decide to simply use his or her bare hands.

Most modern assassinations have been committed either during a public performance or during transport, both because of weaker security and security lapses, such as with US President John F. Kennedy and former Pakistani Prime Minister Benazir Bhutto, or as part of coups d'état where security is either overwhelmed or completely removed, such as with Patrice Lumumba and likely Salvador Allende.

The methods used for protection by famous people have sometimes evoked negative reactions by the public, with some resenting the separation from their officials or major figures. One example might be traveling in a car protected by a bubble of clear bulletproof glass, such as the Popemobile of Pope John Paul II (built following an attempt at his life). Politicians themselves often resent this need for separation – which has at times caused tragedy when they sent their bodyguards from their side for personal or publicity reasons, as U.S. President William McKinley did during the public reception at which he was assassinated.

Other potential targets go into seclusion, and are rarely heard from or seen in public, such as writer Salman Rushdie. A related form of protection is the use of body doubles, a person built similar to the person he is expected to impersonate. These persons are then made up, as well as in some cases altered to look like the target, with the body double then taking the place of the person in high risk situations. According to Joe R. Reeder, Under Secretary of the Army from 1993–1997 writing in Fox News, Fidel Castro had also used body doubles, though no details were specified.

United States Secret Service protective agents receive training in the psychology of assassins.

See also

- Assassinations in fiction
- Contract killing
- List of assassins
- List of assassinated people
- List of unsuccessful assassinations
- List of assassinations and assassination attempts
- List of United States presidential assassination attempts
- Special Activities Division of the Central Intelligence Agency

Further reading

- Porter, Lindsay (2010). *Assassination: a History of Political Murder*. Thames and Hudson. Review [1] The Daily Telegraph, Apr 3, 2010.

External links

- Assassinology.org [2] a website dedicated to the study of assassination
- Notorious Assassinations [3] – slideshow by *Life magazine*
- CNN A short article on the U.S. policy banning political assassination since 1976 [4] from CNN.com/Law Center, November 4, 2002. See also Ford's 1976 executive order [5]. However, Executive Order 12333, which prohibited the CIA from assassinations, was relaxed by the George W. Bush administration.
- Kretzmer, David *"Targeted Killing of Suspected Terrorists: Extra-Judicial Executions or Legitimate Means of Defence?"* [6]. Archived from the original [7] on March 7, 2008. (PDF)
- Is the CIA Assassination Order of a US Citizen Legal? [8] – video by *Democracy Now!*

History of assassination

Assassination, the murder of an opponent or well-known public figure, is one of the oldest tools of power struggles, as well as the expression of certain psychopathic disorders. It dates back to the earliest governments and tribal structures of the world.

Ancient history

Chanakya (c. 350-283 BC) wrote about assassinations in detail in his political treatise *Arthashastra*. His student Chandragupta Maurya, the founder of the Maurya Empire, later made use of assassinations against some of his enemies, including two of Alexander's generals Nicanor and Philip.Wikipedia:WikiProject Disambiguation/Fixing links

Towards the end of the Warring States Period (3rd century BC) in China, the state Qin rose to hegemony over other states. The Prince of the state Yan felt the threat and sought to remove the Qin king (later Qin Shi Huang) and sent Jing Ke for the mission. The assassination attempt was foiled and Jing Ke was killed on the spot.

Leon Czolgosz shoots US President William McKinley in 1901, with a concealed revolver.

The Old Testament story of Judith illustrates how a woman frees the Israelites by tricking and assassinating Holofernes, the war-leader of the enemy Assyrians with whom the Israelites were at war.

Philip II of Macedon, the father of Alexander the Great, can be viewed as a victim of assassination. It is a fact, however, that by the fall of the Roman Republic assassination had become a commonly-accepted tool towards the end not only of improving one's own position, but to influence policy — the killing of Gaius Julius Caesar being a notable example, though many Emperors met such an end. In whatever case, there seems to have not been a good deal of moral indignation at the practice amongst the political circles of the time, save, naturally, by the affected.

As the Middle Ages came about from the fall of the Roman Empire, the moral and ethical dimensions of what was before a simple political tool began to take shape.

Although in that period intentional regicide was an extremely rare occurrence, the situation changed dramatically with the Renaissance when the ideas of *tyrannomachy* (i.e. killing of a King when his rule becomes tyrannical) re-emerged and gained recognition. Several European monarchs and other leading figures were assassinated during religious wars or by religious opponents, for example Henry III and Henry IV of France, and the Protestant Dutch leader, William the Silent. There were also many unsuccessful assassination plots against rulers such as Elizabeth I of England by religious opponents. There were notable detractors, however; Abdülmecid of the Ottoman Empire refused to put to death plotters against his life during his reign.

The Hashshashin, a Muslim group in the Middle Ages-Middle East, was well-known for performing assassinations in the style of close combat. The word *assassin* was derived from the name of their group.

Modern history

Pre-World War I

As the world moved into the present day and the stakes in political clashes of will continued to grow to a global scale, the number of assassinations concurrently multiplied. In Russia alone, five emperors were assassinated within less than 200 years - Ivan VI, Peter III, Paul I, Alexander II and Nicholas II (along with his family: his wife, Alexandra; daughters Olga, Tatiana, Maria and Anastasia, and son Alexey).

Artist's depiction of the assassination of Abraham Lincoln in 1865. From left to right: Henry Rathbone, Clara Harris, Mary Todd Lincoln, Lincoln, and John Wilkes Booth.

The most notable assassination victim within early U.S. history was President Abraham Lincoln. Three other U.S. Presidents have been killed by assassination: James Garfield, William McKinley, and John F. Kennedy. Presidents Andrew Jackson, Franklin D. Roosevelt, Harry S. Truman, Gerald Ford, and Ronald Reagan survived significant assassination attempts (FDR while President-elect, the others while in office). Former President Theodore Roosevelt was shot and wounded during the 1912 presidential campaign. During the Lincoln Assassination, there were also attacks planned against current Vice-president Andrew Johnson and Secretary William H. Seward, but Johnson's did not go through, and Seward survived the attack. An assassination plot against Jefferson Davis, known as the Dahlgren Affair, may have been initiated during the American Civil War.

In Europe the assassination of Archduke Franz Ferdinand by Serb nationalist insurgents triggered World War I.

Post-World War I

However, the 20th century likely marks the first time nation-states began training assassins to be specifically used against so-called enemies of the state. During World War II, for example, MI6 trained a group of Czechoslovakian operatives to kill the Nazi general Reinhard Heydrich (who did later perish by their efforts - see Operation Anthropoid), and repeated attempts were made by both the British MI6, the American Office of Strategic Services (later the Central Intelligence Agency) and the Soviet SMERSH to kill Adolf Hitler, who was in fact nearly killed in a bomb plot by some of his own officers.

India's "Father of the Nation", Mohandas K. Gandhi, was shot on January 30, 1948 by Nathuram Godse, for what Godse perceived as his betrayal of the Hindu cause in attempting to seek peace between Hindus and Muslims.

Cold War and beyond

The Cold War saw a dramatic increase in the number of political assassinations, likely due in large part to the ideological polarization of most of the First and Second worlds, whose adherents were more than willing to both justify and finance such killings. During the Kennedy era Fidel Castro narrowly escaped death on several occasions at the hands of the CIA (a function of the agency's "executive action" program) and CIA-backed rebels (there are accounts that exploding shoes and poisoned clams were employed); some allege that Salvador Allende of Chile was another example, though specific proof is lacking. The assassination of the FBI agent Dan Mitrione, a well known torture's teacher, in hands of the Uruguayan guerrilla movement Tupamaros is a perfect proof of United States intervention in Latin American governments during the Cold War. At the same time, the KGB made creative use of assassination to deal with high-profile defectors such as Georgi Markov, and Israel's Mossad made use of such tactics to eliminate Palestinian guerrillas, politicians and revolutionaries, though some Israelis argue that the targeted often crossed the line between one or another or were even all three. Most major powers were not long in repudiating such tactics, for example during the presidency of Gerald Ford in the United States in 1976 (Executive Order 12333, which proscription was relaxed however by the George W. Bush administration). Many allege, however, that this is merely a smoke screen for political and moral benefit and that the covert and illegal training of assassins by major intelligence agencies continue, such as at the School of the Americas run by the United States. In fact, the debate over the use of such tactics is not closed by any means; many accuse Russia of continuing to practice it in Chechnya and against Chechens abroad, as well as Israel in Palestine and against Palestinians abroad (as well as those Mossad deems a threat to Israeli national security, as in the aftermath of the Munich Massacre during "Operation Wrath of God"). Besides Palestine Liberation Organization members assassinated abroad, Tsahal has also often targeted Hamas activists in the Gaza strip.

Terrorist organizations will frequently target other combatants as well as non-combatants in ther efforts, a prime example was the assassination of Irish solicitor Patrick Finucane who was murdered by the loyalist Ulster Defence Association in 1989 in Belfast, Northern Ireland.

Country-specific

In the Israeli-Palestinian conflict

In the course of the Israeli-Palestinian conflict, the Israel Defense Forces (IDF) employed what they call "focused foiling" (Hebrew: סיכול ממוקד *sikul memukad*) against those suspected by Israel to have intentions of performing a specific act of violence in the very near future or to be linked indirectly with several acts of violence (organizing, planning, researching means of destruction etc.), thus raising the likelihood that his or her assassination would foil similar activities in the future. Usually, such strikes have been carried out by Israeli Air Force attack helicopters that fire guided missiles in the general direction of the target, after the Shin Bet supplies intelligence for the target.

Related controversies

The exact nature of said proof in focused foiling situations is both controversial and classified, as it involves clandestine military intelligence oriented means and operational decisions made by intelligence officers and commanders rather than being a part of a published justice system executed by lawyers and judges.

The IDF says that targeted killings are only pursued to prevent future terrorism acts, not as revenge for past activities however numerous examples indicate otherwise (refer Operation Wrath of God amongst others). It also says that this practice is only used when there is absolutely no practical way of foiling the future acts by other means (e.g., arrest) with minimal risk to the soldiers or civilians. IDF also says that the practice is only used when there is a certainty in the identification of the target, in order to minimize harm to innocent bystanders. These IDF statements have never been monitored or validated by an independent authority, and the IDF deliberations about the killings remain secret. Moreover, actual injury and death of innocent bystanders remains a claim by opponents of these targeted killings.

Defenders of this practice point out that it is in accordance with the Fourth Geneva Convention (Part 3, Article 1, Section 28) which reads: "The presence of a protected person may not be used to render certain points or areas immune from military operations," and so they argue that international law explicitly gives Israel the right to conduct military operations against military targets under these circumstances.

Israeli public support

Targeted killings are largely supported by Israeli society to various extents, but there are exceptions: In 2003, 27 IAF Air Force pilots composed a letter of protest to the Air Force commander Dan Halutz, announcing their refusal to continue and perform attacks on targets within Palestinian population centers, and claiming that the occupation of the Palestinians "morally corrupts the fabric of Israeli society". This letter, the first of its kind emanating from the Air Force, evoked a storm of political protest in Israel, with most circles condemning it as dereliction of duty. IDF ethics forbid soldiers from making public political affiliations, and subsequently the IDF chief of staff announced that all the signatories would be suspended from flight duty, after which some of the pilots recanted and removed their signature.

Well known Israeli operations

Some of the best known targeted killings by Israeli military were Hamas leaders Salah Shahade (July 2002), Sheikh Ahmed Yassin (March 2004), Abdel Aziz al-Rantissi (April 2004) and Adnan al-Ghoul (October 2004). While the term "targeted killing" is mostly used within the context of the Al-Aqsa Intifada by airborne attacks, Israeli security forces have reportedly assassinated top Palestinians in the past, although this was never confirmed officially.

Some of the best known operations include:

- Operation Wrath of God against Black September perpetrators of the 1972 Munich massacre
- Operation Spring of Youth against top PLO leaders in Beirut, Lebanon, 1973
- Abu Jihad (Fatah) in Tunis, 1988
- Fathi Shaqaqi (Palestinian Islamic Jihad) in Malta, 1995
- Yahya Ayyash (Hamas bombmaker, "the engineer") in Gaza, 1996
- Khaled Mashal (Hamas, foiled) in Jordan, 1997

While most assassinations throughout the course of the Israeli-Palestinian conflict were carried out by the IDF against Palestinian leaders of what Israel claims are terror factions, Israeli minister Rehavam Zeevi was assassinated by the Popular Front for the Liberation of Palestine (PFLP), a militant group listed as a terror organization by the U.S. and the EU.

See also: List of Israeli assassinations

Palestinian attacks and Israeli response

Palestinian attacks against Israel have been costly for the Jewish state. IDF reports show that from the start of the Second Intifada (in 2000) to the Year 2005, Palestinians killed 1,074 Israelis and wounded 7,520. These are serious figures for such a small country, roughly equivalent to 50,000 dead and 300,000 wounded in the United States over five years. Such losses generated immense public pressure from the Israeli public for a forceful response, and ramped up targeted killings were one such outcome. While Palestinian operations caused substantial damage, there is also some evidence that the IDF reprisal assassination policy has been salutary in reducing the *effectiveness* of such attacks. As regards Hamas for example, Israeli deaths dropped as the people targeted for assassination were killed, from a high of 75 in 2001, to 21 in 2005. Raw attack figures seem to contradict this result, for Hamas attacks *increased* between 2001 and 2005. Nevertheless, even as the total number of Hamas operations climbed, deaths resulting from such attacks plunged, suggesting that the *effectiveness* of such attacks was being continually weakened.

There are several practical reasons why calculated hits may weaken the effectiveness of terrorist activities. Targeted killings eliminate skilled terrorists, bomb makers, forgers, recruiters and other operatives, who need time to develop expertise. The terror wrought by wildly firing into crowds during 'Targeted hits' also disrupt the opponent's infrastructure and organization and morale, and cause immense stress on the populace, who must constantly move, switch locations and hide. This reduces the flow of information in the terrorist organization and reduces its effectiveness. Assassinations may also serve as a demoralizing agent. Targeted individuals cannot visit their wives, children, relatives or families without severe risk, and may even avoid their names being made public for fear of liquidation. Israeli killings of Hamas leaders Yassin and Rantisi for example, caused Hamas to not publicly identify their replacement, a step necessary to ensure his survival.

Continual diplomatic pressure against the Israeli policy, and the announcement of periodic unilateral cease-fires at various times by Hamas, are seen by some as further proof of the policy's efficacy. Some observers however, argue that other factors are at play besides the hit policy, including improved intelligence gathering leading to more arrests, and the construction of the Israeli security fence which has made it more difficult for terrorist operatives to infiltrate.

United States

In 1943, the United States military used knowledge from decoded transmissions to carry out a targeted killing of the Japanese Admiral Isoroku Yamamoto.

During the Cold War, the United States attempted several times to assassinate Cuban President Fidel Castro.

In 1981, President Ronald Reagan issued Executive Order 12333, which codified a policy first laid down in 1976 by the Ford administration. It stated, "No person employed by or acting on behalf of the United States Government shall engage in, or conspire to engage in, assassination."

In 1986, the American air strikes against Libya included an attack on the barracks where Muammar al-Gaddafi was known to be sleeping. It was claimed that the attack resulted in the death of Qaddafi's infant daughter but reporter Barbara Slavin of USA Today who was in Libya at the time, set the record straight. "His adopted daughter was not killed," she said. "An infant girl was killed. I actually saw her body. She was adopted posthumously by Gadhafi. She was not related to Gadhafi."

During the 1991 Gulf War, the United States struck many of Iraq's most important command bunkers with bunker-busting bombs in hopes of killing Iraqi President Saddam Hussein.[*citation needed*]

Since the rise of al-Qaeda, both the Clinton and Bush administrations have backed "targeted killings." In 1998, in retaliation for the al-Qaeda attacks on U.S. embassies in East Africa, the Clinton administration launched cruise missiles against a training camp in Afghanistan where bin Laden had been hours before. Reportedly, the United States nearly killed the leader of Taliban, Mullah Omar, with a Predator-launched Hellfire missile on the first night of Operation Enduring Freedom. In May 2002, the CIA launched a Hellfire missile from a Predator drone in an effort to kill the Afghan warlord

Gulbuddin Hekmatyar.[citation needed]

On November 3, 2002, a US Central Intelligence Agency-operated MQ-1 Predator unmanned aerial vehicle (UAV) fired a Hellfire missile that destroyed a car carrying six suspected al-Qaeda operatives in Yemen. The target of the attack was Qaed Salim Sinan al-Harethi, the top al-Qaeda operative in Yemen. Among those killed in the attack was a US citizen, Yemeni-American Ahmed Hijazi. Priest, Dana (2002-11-08). "CIA Killed U.S. Citizen In Yemen Missile Strike" [1]. *Washington Post*. Retrieved 2008-02-28. [citation needed]

According to Bush administration, the killing of an American in this fashion was legal. "I can assure you that no constitutional questions are raised here. There are authorities that the president can give to officials. He's well within the balance of accepted practice and the letter of his constitutional authority," said Condoleezza Rice, the US national security adviser.

During the press-conference, the US State Department spokesman Richard Boucher said that Washington's reasons for opposing the targeted killings of Palestinians might not apply in other circumstances and denied allegation that by staging the Yemen operation the US may be using double standards towards Israeli policy: "We all understand the situation with regard to Israeli-Palestinian issues and the prospects of peace and the prospects of negotiation... and of the need to create an atmosphere for progress... A lot of different things come into play there... Our policy on targeted killings in the Israeli-Palestinian context has not changed."

On December 3, 2005, the US was blamed for another incident, in which alleged al-Qaeda #3 man (operations chief Abu Hamza Rabia) was reportedly killed in Pakistan by an airborne missile, together with four associates. However, Pakistani officials claim the group was killed while preparing explosives, not from any targeted military operation., The US has made no official comment about the incident.

On January 13, 2006 US CIA-operated unmanned Predator drones launched four Hellfire missiles into the Pakistani village of Damadola, about 7 km (4.5 miles) from the Afghan border, killing at least 18 people. The attack targeted Ayman al-Zawahiri who was thought to be in the village. Pakistani officials later said that al-Zawahiri was not there and that the U.S. had acted on faulty intelligence.

On June 7, 2006, US Forces dropped one laser-guided bomb and one GPS-guided bomb on a safehouse north of Baqubah, Iraq, where Al-Qaeda in Iraq leader Abu Musab al-Zarqawi was believed to be meeting with several aides. His death was confirmed the next day.

See also: War on Terrorism

Russia (post-communism)

Russia employed similar strategy in the course of its First and Second Chechen Wars, targeting the leaders of separatist movement. Chechen President Dzhokhar Dudaev was killed by an air strike of Russian Air Force on April 21, 1996 and Aslan Maskhadov was killed on March 8, 2005. On July 10, 2006, Shamil Basayev, the Chechen rebel, was killed in an explosion—though it is unclear if this was an accident in the handling of explosives, or a targeted Russian attack.

"When terrorists feel they are literally being trailed, fighting groups are systematically being detained, when in fact a top leader is eliminated, this creates an atmosphere in which there's no place for terrorist attacks," said Vladimir Vasilyev, head of the security committee of the lower house of the Russian State Duma.

The First Attempt on A President

Richard Lawrence (failed assassin)

Richard Lawrence (1800? – June 13, 1861) is the first known person to attempt to assassinate an American President —Andrew Jackson. Lawrence was born in England in 1800 or 1801. By the time he reached adulthood he was considered mentally ill.

The etching of the assassination attempt.

Life

Lawrence worked as a painter and there is speculation that exposure to the chemicals in his paints may have contributed to his derangement. By the early 1830s he was unemployed and had succumbed to the delusion that he was King Richard III of England.

His personality changed dramatically around this point. He was previously conservatively dressed, but now he dressed flamboyantly, and grew a mustache. He gave up his job, saying that he had no need to work as the American government owed him a large sum of money but that President Andrew Jackson was keeping him from receiving it. He also said that when he received the money, he could take up his rightful place as King of England. Lawrence also blamed Jackson for killing his father in 1832, despite the fact that Lawrence's father had died nine years earlier and had never been to the United States.

Assassination attempt

Lawrence decided he should kill Jackson. He purchased two pistols and began observing Jackson's movements. For several weeks before the assassination attempt, he was seen on most days in the same paint shop, repeatedly talking and laughing to himself. On January 30, 1835, Jackson was attending the funeral of South Carolina congressman Warren R. Davis. Lawrence originally planned to shoot Jackson as he entered the service but was unable to get close enough to the President. However when Jackson left the funeral, Lawrence had found a space near a pillar where Jackson would pass. As Jackson walked, Lawrence stepped out and fired his first pistol at Jackson's back; it misfired. Lawrence quickly made another attempt with his second pistol but that also misfired. It was later determined that the weapons he had chosen were noted for being vulnerable to moisture and the weather on that date was extremely humid.

Lawrence's unsuccessful attempts had drawn the attention of the crowd and he was quickly wrestled into submission by those present (including Congressman Davy Crockett). It is reported that Jackson assisted in subduing his attempted assassin, striking him several times with his cane.

Trial and commitment

Lawrence was brought to trial on April 11, 1835. The prosecuting attorney was Francis Scott Key. After only five minutes of deliberation, the jury found Lawrence not guilty by reason of insanity. In the years following his conviction, Lawrence was held by several institutions and hospitals. In 1855, he was committed to the newly-opened Government Hospital for the Insane (later renamed St. Elizabeths Hospital) in Washington, D.C. where he remained until his death in 1861.

Aftermath

As with later assassinations, there would be speculation that Lawrence was part of a conspiracy. While nobody denied Lawrence's involvement, many people, including Jackson, believed that he may have been supported or put up to carrying out the assassination attempt by the President's political enemies. Senator John C. Calhoun made a statement on the U.S. Senate floor that he was not connected to the attack. Jackson believed Calhoun, an old enemy of his, was at the bottom of the attempt. Jackson also suspected a former friend and supporter, Senator George Poindexter of Mississippi, who had used Lawrence to do some house painting a few months earlier. Poindexter was unable to convince his supporters in Mississippi that he was not involved in a plot against the President, and was defeated for reelection. All subsequent evidence indicates that Lawrence was a deranged man acting alone most likely due to paranoid schizophrenic delusions.

External links

- American Heritage Article on Richard Lawrence's Assassination Attempt [1]

The Death of A President

John Wilkes Booth

	John Wilkes Booth

	John Wilkes Booth
Born	May 10, 1838 Bel Air, Maryland, U.S.A.
Died	April 26, 1865 (aged 26) Port Royal, Virginia, U.S.A.
Occupation	Actor
Known for	Assassination of Abraham Lincoln
Religion	Protestant Episcopal
Parents	Junius Brutus Booth and Mary Ann Holmes
Signature	
	J. Wilkes Booth

John Wilkes Booth (May 10, 1838– April 26, 1865) was an American stage actor who assassinated President Abraham Lincoln at Ford's Theatre, in Washington, D.C., on April 14, 1865. Booth was a member of the prominent 19th century Booth theatrical family from Maryland and, by the 1860s, was a well known actor. He was also a Confederate sympathizer vehement in his denunciation of the Lincoln Administration and outraged by the South's defeat in the American Civil War. He strongly opposed the abolition of slavery in the United States and Lincoln's proposal to extend voting rights to recently emancipated slaves.

Booth and a group of co-conspirators planned to kill Lincoln, Vice President Andrew Johnson, and Secretary of State William Seward in a bid to help the Confederacy's cause. Although Robert E. Lee's Army of Northern Virginia had surrendered four days earlier, Booth believed the war was not yet over because Confederate General Joseph E. Johnston's army was still fighting the Union Army. Of the conspirators, only Booth was completely successful in carrying out his part of the plot. Seward was wounded but recovered; Lincoln died the next morning from a single gunshot wound to the back of the head – altering the course of American history in the aftermath of the Civil War.

Following the shooting, Booth fled on horseback to southern Maryland. He eventually made his way to a farm in rural northern Virginia; he was tracked down and shot by Union soldiers 12 days later. Eight others were tried and convicted, and four were hanged shortly thereafter. Over the years, various authors have suggested that Booth might have escaped his pursuers and subsequently died many years later under a pseudonym.

Background and early life

Booth's parents, the noted British Shakespearean actor Junius Brutus Booth and his mistress Mary Ann Holmes, came to the United States from England in June 1821. They purchased a 150-acre (61 ha) farm near Bel Air in Harford County, Maryland, where John Wilkes Booth was born in a four-room log house on May 10, 1838, the ninth of ten children. He was named after the English radical politician John Wilkes, a distant relative. Junius Brutus Booth's wife, Adelaide Delannoy Booth, was granted a divorce in 1851 on grounds of adultery, and Holmes legally wed John Wilkes Booth's father on May 10, 1851, the youth's 13th birthday. Booth's father built Tudor Hall that year on the Harford County property as the family's summer home, while also maintaining a winter residence on Exeter Street in Baltimore in the 1840s–1850s.

"Tudor Hall" in 1865

As a boy, John Wilkes Booth was athletic and popular, becoming skilled at horsemanship and fencing. A sometimes indifferent student, he attended the Bel Air Academy, where the headmaster described him as "[n]ot deficient in intelligence, but disinclined to take advantage of the educational opportunities offered him". Each day he rode back and forth from farm to school, taking more interest in what happened along the way than in reaching his classes on time".
In 1850–1851, he attended the Quaker-run Milton Boarding School for Boys located in Sparks, Maryland, and later St. Timothy's Hall, an Episcopal military academy in Catonsville, Maryland, beginning when he was 13 years old. At the Milton school, students recited such classical works as those by Herodotus, Cicero, and Tacitus. Students at St. Timothy's wore military uniforms and were subject to a regimen of daily formation drills and strict discipline. Booth left school at 14, after his father's death.

While attending the Milton Boarding School, Booth met a Gypsy fortune-teller who read his palm and pronounced a grim destiny, telling Booth that he would have a grand but short life, doomed to die young and "meeting a bad end". His sister recalled that Booth wrote down the palm-reader's prediction and showed it to his family and others, often discussing its portents in moments of melancholy in later years.

As recounted by Booth's sister, Asia Booth Clarke, in her memoirs written in 1874, no one church was preeminent in the Booth household. Booth's mother was Episcopalian and his father was described as a free spirit, preferring a Sunday walk along the Baltimore waterfront with his children to attending church. On January 23, 1853, the 14-year-old Booth was finally baptized at St. Timothy's Protestant Episcopal Church.

By the age of 16, Booth was interested in the theatre and in politics, becoming a delegate from Bel Air to a rally by the Know Nothing Party for Henry Winter Davis, the anti-immigrant party's candidate for Congress in the 1854 elections. Aspiring to follow in the footsteps of his father and his actor brothers, Edwin and Junius Brutus, Jr., Booth began practicing elocution daily in the woods around Tudor Hall and studying Shakespeare.

Theatrical career

1850s

At age 17, Booth made his stage debut on August 14, 1855, in the supporting role of the Earl of Richmond in *Richard III* at Baltimore's Charles Street Theatre. The audience hissed at the inexperienced actor when he missed some of his lines. He also began acting at Baltimore's Holliday Street Theater, owned by John T. Ford, where the Booths had performed frequently. In 1857, Booth joined the stock company of the Arch Street Theatre in Philadelphia, Pennsylvania, where he played for a full season. At his request he was billed as "J.B. Wilkes", a pseudonym meant to avoid comparison with other members of his famous thespian family. Author Jim Bishop wrote that

The Richmond Theatre, Richmond, Virginia, in 1858, when Booth made his first stage appearance there

Booth "developed into an outrageous scene stealer, but he played his parts with such heightened enthusiasm that the audiences idolized him." In February 1858, he played in *Lucrezia Borgia* at the Arch Street Theatre. On opening night, he experienced stage fright and stumbled over his line. Instead of introducing himself by saying, "Madame, I am Petruchio Pandolfo", he stammered, "Madame, I am Pondolfio Pet—Pedolfio Pat—Pantuchio Ped—dammit! Who am I?", causing the audience to roar with laughter.

Later that year, Booth played the part of an Indian, Uncas, in a play staged in Petersburg, Virginia, and then became a stock company actor at the Richmond Theatre in Virginia, where he became increasingly popular with audiences for his energetic performances. On October 5, 1858, Booth played the part of Horatio in *Hamlet*, with his older brother Edwin having the title role. Afterward, Edwin led the younger Booth to the theatre's footlights and said to the audience, "I think he's done well, don't you?" In response, the audience applauded loudly and cried "Yes! Yes!" In all, John Wilkes performed in 83 plays in 1858. Among them were William Wallace and Brutus, having as their theme the killing or overthrow of an unjust ruler. Booth said that of all Shakespearean characters, his favorite role was Brutus – the slayer of a tyrant.

Some critics called Booth "the handsomest man in America" and a "natural genius" and noted his having an "astonishing memory"; others were mixed in their estimation of his acting. He stood 5 feet 8 inches (1.73 m) tall, had jet-black hair, and was lean and athletic. Noted Civil War reporter George Alfred Townsend described him as a "muscular, perfect man", with "curling hair, like a Corinthian capital".

Booth's stage performances were often characterized by his contemporaries as acrobatic and intensely physical, leaping upon the stage and gesturing with passion. He was an excellent swordsman, although a fellow actor once recalled that he occasionally cut himself with his own sword.

Historian Benjamin Platt Thomas wrote that Booth "won celebrity with theater-goers by his romantic personal attraction", but that he was "too impatient for hard study" and his "brilliant talents had failed of full development. Author Gene Smith wrote that Booth's acting may not have been as precise as his brother Edwin's, but his strikingly handsome appearance enthralled women. As the 1850s drew to a close, Booth was becoming wealthy as an actor, earning $20,000 a year (equivalent to more than $500,000 in 2009).

1860s

After finishing the 1859–1860 theatre season in Richmond, Virginia, Booth embarked on his first national tour as a leading actor. He engaged a Philadelphia attorney, Matthew Canning, to serve as his agent. By mid-1860, he was playing in such cities as New York, Boston, Chicago, Cleveland, St. Louis, Columbus, Georgia, Montgomery, Alabama, and New Orleans. Poet and journalist Walt Whitman said of Booth's acting, "He would have flashes, passages, I thought of real genius". The *Philadelphia Press* drama critic said, "Without having [his brother] Edwin's culture and grace, Mr. Booth has far more action, more life, and, we are inclined to think, more natural genius."

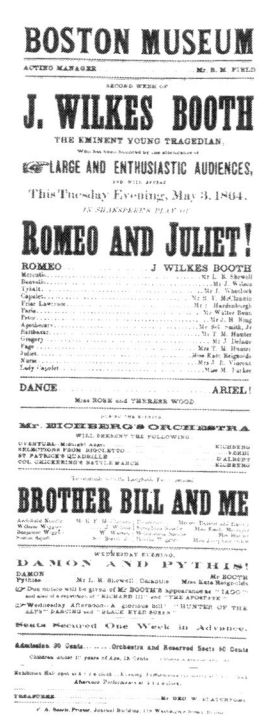

Boston Museum playbill advertising Booth in *Romeo and Juliet*, May 3, 1864

When the Civil War began on April 12, 1861, Booth was starring in Albany, New York. His outspoken admiration for the South's secession, publicly calling it "heroic", so enraged local citizens that they demanded his banning from the stage for making "treasonable statements". Albany's drama critics were kinder, however, giving him rave reviews. One called him a genius, praising his acting for "never fail[ing] to delight with his masterly impressions". As the Civil War raged across the divided land in 1862, Booth appeared mostly in Union and border states. In January, he played the title role in *Richard III* in St. Louis and then made his Chicago debut. In March, he made his first acting appearance in New York City. In May 1862, he made his Boston debut, playing nightly at the Boston Museum in *Richard III* (May 12, 15, and 23), *Romeo and Juliet* (May 13), *The Robbers* (May 14 and 21), *Hamlet* (May 16), *The Apostate* (May 19), *The Stranger* (May 20), and *The Lady of Lyons* (May 22). Following his performance of *Richard III* on May 12, the Boston *Transcript*'s review the next day called Booth "the most promising young actor on the American stage".

Starting in January 1863, he returned to the Boston Museum for a series of plays, including the role of the villain Duke Pescara in *The Apostate* that won acclaim from audiences and critics. Back in Washington in April, he played the title roles in *Hamlet* and *Richard III*, one of his favorites. Billed as "The Pride of the American People, A Star of the First Magnitude", the critics were equally enthusiastic. The *National Republican* drama critic said Booth "took the hearts of the audience by storm" and termed his performance "a complete triumph". At the beginning of July 1863, Booth finished the acting season at Cleveland's Academy of Music, as the Battle of Gettysburg raged in Pennsylvania. Between September–November 1863, Booth played a hectic schedule in the northeast, appearing in Boston, Providence, Rhode Island, and Hartford, Connecticut. Each day he received fan mail from infatuated women.

When family friend John T. Ford opened 1,500-seat Ford's Theatre on November 9 in Washington, D.C., Booth was one of the first leading men to appear there, playing in Charles Selby's *The Marble Heart*. In this play, Booth portrayed a Greek sculptor in costume, making marble statues come to life. Lincoln watched the play from his box. At one point during the performance, Booth was said to have shaken his finger in Lincoln's direction as he delivered a line of dialogue. Lincoln's sister-in-law, sitting with him in the same presidential box where he would later be slain, turned to him and said, "Mr. Lincoln, he looks as if he meant that for you." The President replied, "He does look pretty sharp at me, doesn't he?" On another occasion when Lincoln's son Tad saw Booth perform, he said the actor thrilled him, prompting Booth to give the President's youngest son a rose. Booth ignored an invitation to visit

Lincoln between acts, however.

On November 25, 1864, Booth performed for the only time with his two brothers, Edwin and Junius, in a single engagement production of *Julius Caesar* at the Winter Garden Theatre in New York. He played Mark Antony and his brother Edwin had the larger role of Brutus in a performance acclaimed as "the greatest theatrical event in New York history". The proceeds went towards a statue of William Shakespeare for Central Park, which still stands today. In January 1865, he acted in Shakespeare's *Romeo and Juliet* in Washington, again garnering rave reviews. The *National Intelligencer* enthused of Booth's Romeo, "the most satisfactory of all renderings of that fine character", especially praising the death scene. Booth made the final appearance of his acting career at Ford's on March 18, 1865, when he again played Duke Pescara in *The Apostate*.

L-to-r: Booth with brothers Edwin and Junius in *Julius Caesar*

Business ventures

Booth invested some of his growing wealth in various enterprises during the early 1860s, including land speculation in Boston's Back Bay section. He also started a business partnership with John Ellsler, manager of the Cleveland Academy of Music, and another friend, Thomas Mears, to develop oil wells in northwestern Pennsylvania, where an oil boom had started in August 1859, following Edwin Drake's discovery of oil there. Initially calling their venture Dramatic Oil (later renaming it Fuller Farm Oil), the partners invested in a 31.5-acre (12.7 ha) site along the Allegheny River at Franklin, Pennsylvania, in late 1863 for drilling. By early 1864, they had a producing 1900-foot (579 m) deep oil well, named Wilhelmina for Mears' wife, yielding 25 barrels (4 kL) of crude oil daily, then considered a good yield. The Fuller Farm Oil company was selling shares with a prospectus featuring the well-known actor's celebrity status as "Mr. J. Wilkes Booth, a successful and intelligent operator in oil lands", it said. The partners, impatient to increase the well's output, attempted the use of explosives, which wrecked the well and ended production. Booth, already growing more obsessed with the South's worsening situation in the Civil War and angered at Lincoln's re-election, withdrew from the oil business on November 27, 1864, with a substantial loss of his $6,000 ($81,400 in 2010 dollars) investment.

Civil War years

Strongly opposed to the abolitionists who sought to end slavery in the U.S., Booth attended the hanging on December 2, 1859, of abolitionist leader John Brown, who was executed for leading a raid on the Federal armory at Harpers Ferry (in present-day West Virginia). Booth had been rehearsing at the Richmond Theatre when he abruptly decided to join the Richmond Grays, a volunteer militia of 1,500 men travelling to Charles Town for Brown's hanging, to guard against an attempt by abolitionists to rescue Brown from the gallows by force. When Brown was hanged without incident, Booth stood in uniform near the scaffold and afterwards expressed great satisfaction with Brown's fate, although he admired the condemned man's bravery in facing death stoically.

Lincoln was elected president on November 6, 1860, and the following month Booth drafted a long speech, apparently undelivered, that decried Northern abolitionism and made clear his strong support of the South and the institution of slavery. On April 12, 1861, the Civil War began, and eventually 11 Southern states seceded from the Union. In Booth's native Maryland, the slaveholding portion of the population favored joining the Confederate States of America. Because the threatened secession of Maryland would leave the Federal capital of Washington, D.C., an indefensible enclave within the Confederacy, Lincoln suspended the writ of *habeas corpus* and imposed martial law in Baltimore and portions of the state, ordering the imprisonment of pro-secession Maryland political leaders at Ft. McHenry and the stationing of Federal troops in Baltimore. Although Maryland remained in the Union, newspaper editorials and many Marylanders, including Booth, agreed with Supreme Court Chief Justice Roger B. Taney's decision in *Ex parte Merryman* that Lincoln's actions were unconstitutional.

As a popular actor in the 1860s, he continued to travel extensively to perform in the North and South, and as far west as New Orleans, Louisiana. According to his sister Asia, Booth confided to her that he also used his position to smuggle quinine to the South during his travels there, helping the Confederacy obtain the needed drug despite the Northern blockade.

Although Booth was pro-Confederate, his family, like many Marylanders, was divided. He was outspoken in his love of the South, and equally outspoken in his hatred of Lincoln. As the Civil War went on, Booth increasingly quarreled with his brother Edwin, who declined to make stage appearances in the South and refused to listen to John Wilkes' fiercely partisan denunciations of the North and Lincoln. In early 1863, Booth was arrested in St. Louis while on a theatre tour, when he was heard saying he "wished the President and the whole damned government would go to hell". Charged with making "treasonous" remarks against the government, he was released when he took an oath of allegiance to the Union and paid a substantial fine.

Lucy Lambert Hale, Booth's fiancée in 1865

John Wilkes Booth

In February 1865, Booth became infatuated with Lucy Lambert Hale, the daughter of U.S. Senator John P. Hale of New Hampshire, and they became secretly engaged when Booth received his mother's blessing for their marriage plans. "You have so often been dead in love," his mother counseled Booth in a letter, "be well assured she is really and truly devoted to you." Booth composed a handwritten Valentine card for his fiancée on February 13, expressing his "adoration". She was unaware of Booth's deep antipathy towards President Lincoln.

Plot to kidnap Lincoln

As the 1864 Presidential election drew near, the Confederacy's prospects for victory were ebbing and the tide of war increasingly favored the North. The likelihood of Lincoln's re-election filled Booth with rage towards the President, whom Booth blamed for the war and all the South's troubles. Booth, who had promised his mother at the outbreak of war that he would not enlist as a soldier, increasingly chafed at not fighting for the South, confiding in his diary, "I have begun to deem myself a coward and to despise my own existence". He began to formulate plans to kidnap Lincoln from his summer residence at the Old Soldiers Home, three miles (5 km) from the White House, and to smuggle him across the Potomac River into Richmond. Once in Confederate hands, Lincoln would be exchanged for the release of Confederate Army prisoners of war held captive in Northern prisons and, Booth reasoned, bring the war to an end by emboldening opposition to the war in the North or forcing Union recognition of the Confederate government.

Throughout the Civil War, the Confederacy maintained a network of underground operators in southern Maryland, particularly Charles and St. Mary's counties, smuggling recruits across the Potomac River into Virginia and relaying messages for Confederate agents as far north as Canada. Booth recruited his friends Samuel Arnold and Michael O'Laughlen as accomplices. They met often at the house of Maggie Branson, a known Confederate sympathizer, at 16 North Eutaw Street in Baltimore. He also met with several well-known Confederate sympathizers at The Parker House in Boston.

The Old Soldiers Home, where Booth planned to kidnap Lincoln

In October, Booth made an unexplained trip to Montreal, which was then a well-known center of clandestine Confederate activity. He spent 10 days in the city, staying for a time at St. Lawrence Hall, a rendezvous for the Confederate Secret Service, and meeting several Confederate agents there. No conclusive proof has linked Booth's kidnapping or assassination plots to a conspiracy involving the leadership of the Confederate government, although historians such as David Herbert Donald have said, "It is clear that, at least at the lower levels of the Southern secret service, the abduction of the Union President was under consideration". Historian Thomas Goodrich concluded that Booth entered the Confederate Secret Service as a spy and courier. Other writers exploring possible connections between Booth's planning and Confederate agents include Nathan Miller's *Spying For America* and William Tidwell's *Come Retribution: the Confederate Secret Service and the Assassination of Lincoln.*

After Lincoln's landslide re-election in early November 1864 on a platform advocating passage of the 13th Amendment to the U.S. Constitution to abolish slavery altogether, Booth devoted increasing energy and money to his kidnap plot. He assembled a loose-knit band of Southern sympathizers, including David Herold, George Atzerodt, Lewis Powell (also known as Lewis Payne or Paine), and John Surratt, a rebel agent. They began to meet routinely at the boarding house of Surratt's mother, Mrs. Mary Surratt.

By this time, Booth was arguing so vehemently with his older, pro-Union brother Edwin about Lincoln and the war that Edwin finally told him he was no longer welcome at his New York home. Booth also railed against Lincoln in conversations with his sister Asia, saying, "That man's appearance, his pedigree, his coarse low jokes and anecdotes, his vulgar similes, and his policy are a disgrace to the seat he holds. He is made the tool of the North, to crush out slavery." As the Confederacy's defeat became more certain in 1865, Booth decried the end of slavery and Lincoln's election to a second term, "making himself a king", the actor fumed, in "wild tirades", his sister recalled.

Booth attended Lincoln's second inauguration on March 4 as the invited guest of his secret fiancée, Lucy Hale. In the crowd below were Powell, Atzerodt, and Herold. There was no attempt to assassinate Lincoln during the inauguration. Later, however, Booth remarked about his "excellent chance ... to kill the President, if I had wished".

On March 17, Booth learned that Lincoln would be attending a performance of the play *Still Waters Run Deep* at a hospital near the Soldier's Home. Booth assembled his team on a stretch of road near the Soldier's Home in the attempt to kidnap Lincoln en route to the hospital, but the president did not appear. Booth later learned that Lincoln had changed his plans at the last moment to attend a reception at the National Hotel in Washington where, coincidentally, Booth was then staying.

Assassination of Lincoln

Main article: Abraham Lincoln assassination

On April 12, 1865, after hearing the news that Robert E. Lee had surrendered at Appomattox Court House, Booth told Louis J. Weichmann, a friend of John Surratt, and a boarder at Mary Surratt's house, that he was done with the stage and that the only play he wanted to present henceforth was *Venice Preserv'd*. Weichmann did not understand the reference: *Venice Preserv'd* is about an assassination plot. With the Union Army's capture of Richmond and Lee's surrender, Booth's scheme to kidnap Lincoln was no longer feasible, and he changed his goal to assassination.

The previous day, Booth was in the crowd outside the White House when Lincoln gave an impromptu speech from his window. When Lincoln stated that he was in favor of granting suffrage to the former slaves, Booth declared that it would be the last speech Lincoln would ever make.

On the morning of Good Friday, April 14, 1865, Booth went to Ford's Theatre to get his mail, where he was told by John Ford's brother that President and Mrs. Lincoln accompanied by Gen. and Mrs. Ulysses S. Grant would be attending the play *Our American Cousin* at Ford's Theatre that evening. He immediately set about making plans for the assassination, which included making arrangements with livery stable owner James W. Pumphrey for a getaway horse, and an escape route. Booth informed Powell, Herold, and Atzerodt of his intention to kill Lincoln. He assigned Powell to assassinate Secretary of State William H. Seward and Atzerodt to assassinate Vice President Andrew Johnson. Herold would assist in their escape into Virginia.

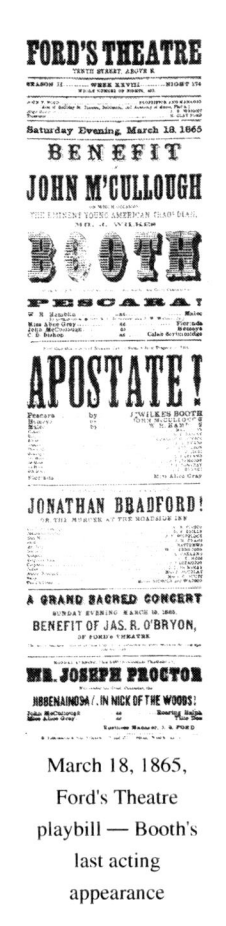

March 18, 1865, Ford's Theatre playbill — Booth's last acting appearance

By targeting Lincoln and his two immediate successors to the presidency, Booth seems to have intended to decapitate the Union government and throw it into a state of panic and confusion. The possibility of assassinating the Union Army's commanding general as well was foiled when Grant declined the theatre invitation at his wife's insistence. Instead, the Grants departed Washington by train that evening for a visit to relatives in New Jersey. Booth had hoped that the assassinations would create sufficient chaos within the Union that the Confederate government could reorganize and continue the war if one Confederate army remained in the field or, that failing, to avenge the South's defeat. In his 2005 analysis of Lincoln's assassination, Thomas Goodrich wrote, "All the elements in Booth's nature came together at once – his hatred of tyranny, his love of liberty, his passion for the stage, his sense of drama, and his lifelong quest to become immortal."

As a famous and popular actor who had frequently performed at Ford's Theatre, and who was well known to its owner, John T. Ford, Booth had free access to all parts of the theater, even having his mail sent there. By boring a spyhole into the door of the presidential box earlier that day, the assassin could check that his intended victim had made it to the play and observe the box's occupants. That evening, at around 10 p.m., as the play progressed, John Wilkes Booth slipped into Lincoln's box and shot him in the back of the head with a .44 caliber Derringer. Booth's escape was almost thwarted by Major Henry Rathbone, who was present in the Presidential box with Mrs. Mary Todd Lincoln. Booth stabbed Rathbone when the startled officer lunged at him. Rathbone's fiancée, Clara Harris, who was also present in the box, was unhurt.

Currier and Ives depiction of Lincoln's assassination. *L-to-r:* Maj. Rathbone, Clara Harris, Mary Todd Lincoln, Pres. Lincoln, and Booth

Booth then jumped from the President's box to the stage, where he raised his knife and shouted "*Sic semper tyrannis*" (Latin for "Thus always to tyrants", attributed to Brutus at Caesar's assassination and the Virginia state motto), while others said he added, "I have done it, the South is avenged!" Various accounts state that Booth injured his leg when his spur snagged a decorative U.S. Treasury Guard flag while leaping to the stage. Historian Michael W. Kauffman questioned this legend in his book, *American Brutus: John Wilkes Booth and the Lincoln Conspiracies*, writing in 2004 that eyewitness accounts of Booth's hurried stage exit made it unlikely that his leg was broken then. Kauffman contends that Booth was injured later that night during his flight to escape when his horse tripped and fell on him, calling Booth's claim to the contrary an exaggeration to portray his own actions as heroic.

Booth was the only one of the assassins to succeed. Powell was able to stab Seward, who was bedridden as a result of an earlier carriage accident; although badly wounded, Seward survived. Atzerodt lost his nerve and spent the evening drinking; he never made an attempt on Johnson's life.

Reaction and pursuit

In the ensuing pandemonium inside Ford's Theatre, Booth fled by a stage door to the alley, where his getaway horse was held for him by Joseph "Peanuts" Burroughs. The owner of the horse had warned Booth that the horse was high spirited and would break halter if left unattended. Booth left the horse with Edmund Spangler and Spangler arranged for Burroughs to hold the horse.

The fleeing assassin galloped into southern Maryland, accompanied by David Herold, having planned his escape route to take advantage of the sparsely-settled area's lack of telegraphs and railroads, along with its predominantly Confederate sympathies. He thought that the area's dense forests and swampy terrain of Zekiah Swamp made it ideal for an escape route into rural Virginia. At midnight, Booth and Herold arrived at Surratt's Tavern on the Brandywine Pike, 9 miles (14 km) from Washington, where they had stored guns and equipment earlier in the year as part of the kidnap plot.

The fugitives then continued southward, stopping before dawn on April 15 at the home of Dr. Samuel Mudd, 25 miles (40 km) from Washington, for treatment of Booth's injured leg. Mudd later said that Booth told him the injury occurred when his horse fell. The next day, Booth and Herold arrived at the home of Samuel Cox around 4 a.m. As the two fugitives hid in the woods nearby, Cox contacted Thomas A. Jones, his foster brother and a Confederate agent in charge of spy operations in the southern Maryland area since 1862. By order of Secretary of War Edwin M. Stanton, the War Department advertised a $100,000 reward for information leading to the arrest of Booth and his accomplices, and Federal troops were dispatched to search southern Maryland extensively, following tips reported by Federal intelligence agents to Col. Lafayette Baker.

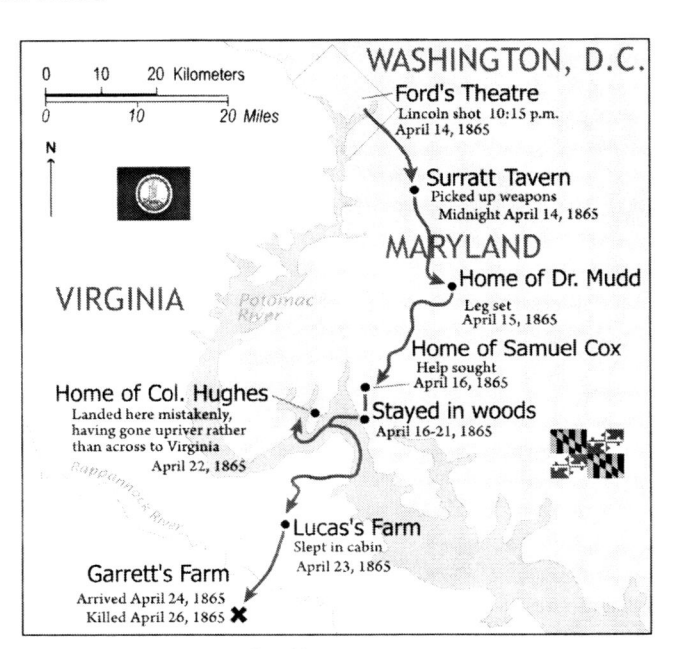

While Federal troops combed the rural area's woods and swamps for Booth in the days following the assassination, the nation experienced an outpouring of grief. On April 18, mourners waited seven abreast in a mile-long line outside the White House for the public viewing of the slain president, reposing in his open walnut casket in the black-draped East Room. A cross of lilies was at the head and roses covered the coffin's lower half. Thousands of mourners arriving on special trains jammed Washington for the next day's funeral, sleeping on hotel floors and even resorting to blankets spread outdoors on the capital's lawn. Prominent abolitionist leader and orator Frederick Douglass called the assassination an "unspeakable calamity" for African-Americans. Great indignation was directed towards Booth as the assassin's identity was telegraphed across the nation. Newspapers called him an "accursed devil", "monster", "madman", and a "wretched fiend". Historian Dorothy Kunhardt wrote: "Almost every family who kept a photograph album on the parlor table owned a likeness of John Wilkes Booth of the famous Booth family of actors. After the assassination Northerners slid the Booth card out of their albums: some threw it away, some burned it, some crumpled it angrily." Even in the South, sorrow was expressed in some quarters. In Savannah, Georgia, where the mayor and city council addressed a vast throng at an outdoor gathering to express their indignation, many in the crowd wept. Confederate Gen. Joseph E. Johnston called Booth's act "a disgrace to the age". Robert E. Lee also expressed regret at Lincoln's death by Booth's hand.

Not all were grief-stricken, however. In New York City, a man was attacked by an enraged crowd when he shouted, "It served Old Abe right!" after hearing the news of Lincoln's death. Elsewhere in the South, Lincoln was hated in death as in life, and Booth was viewed as a hero as many rejoiced at news of his deed. Other Southerners feared that a vengeful North would exact a terrible retribution upon the defeated former Confederate states. "Instead of being a great Southern hero, his deed was considered the worst possible tragedy that could have befallen the South as well as the North", wrote Kunhardt.

While hiding in the Maryland woods as he waited for an opportunity to cross the Potomac River into Virginia, Booth read the accounts of national mourning reported in the newspapers brought to him by Jones each day. By April 20, he was aware that some of his co-conspirators were already arrested: Mary Surratt, Powell (or Paine), Arnold, and O'Laughlen. Booth was surprised to find little public sympathy for his action, especially from those anti-Lincoln newspapers that had previously excoriated the President in life. As news of the assassination reached the far corners of the nation, indignation was aroused against Lincoln's critics, whom many blamed for encouraging Booth to act. The *San Francisco Chronicle* editorialized: "Booth has simply carried out what ... secession politicians and journalists have been for years expressing in words ... who have denounced the President as a 'tyrant', a 'despot', a 'usurper', hinted at, and virtually recommended." Booth wrote of his dismay in a journal entry on April 21, as he awaited nightfall before crossing the Potomac River into Virginia (*see map*):

> "For six months we had worked to capture. But our cause being almost lost, something decisive and great must be done. I struck boldly, and not as the papers say. I can never repent it, though we hated to kill."

That same day, the nine-car funeral train bearing Lincoln's body departed Washington on the Baltimore and Ohio Railroad, arriving at Baltimore's Camden Station at 10 a.m., the first stop on a 13-day journey to Springfield, Illinois, its final destination. As the funeral train slowly made its way westward through seven states, stopping en route at Harrisburg, Philadelphia, Trenton, New York, Albany, Buffalo, Cleveland, Columbus, Ohio, Cincinnati, and Indianapolis during the following days, 30 million people lined the railroad tracks along the 1662-mile (2675 km) route, holding aloft signs with legends such as "We mourn our loss", "He lives in the hearts of his people", and "The darkest hour in history".

Broadside advertising reward for capture of Lincoln assassination conspirators, illustrated with photographic prints of John H. Surratt, John Wilkes Booth, and David E. Herold.

In the cities where the train stopped, 1.5 million people viewed Lincoln in his coffin. Aboard the train was Clarence Depew, president of the New York Central Railroad, who said, "As we sped over the rails at night, the scene was the most pathetic ever witnessed. At every crossroads the glare of innumerable torches illuminated the whole population, kneeling on the ground." Dorothy Kunhardt called the funeral train's journey "the mightiest outpouring of national grief the world had yet seen".

Meanwhile, as mourners were viewing Lincoln's remains when the funeral train steamed into Harrisburg at 8:20 p.m., Booth and Herold were provided with a boat and compass by Jones, to cross the Potomac at night on April 21. Instead of reaching Virginia, however, they mistakenly navigated upriver to a bend in the broad Potomac River, coming ashore again in Maryland on April 22. The 23-year old Herold knew the area well, having frequently hunted there, and recognized a nearby farm as belonging to a Confederate sympathizer. The farmer led them to his son-in-law, Col. John J. Hughes, who provided the fugitives with food and a hideout until nightfall, for a second attempt to row across the river to Virginia. Booth wrote in his diary, "With every man's hand against me, I am here in despair. And why; For doing what Brutus was honored for ... And yet I for striking down a greater tyrant than they ever knew am looked upon as a common cutthroat." The pair finally reached the Virginia shore near Machodoc Creek before dawn on April 23. There, they made contact with Thomas Harbin, whom Booth had previously brought into his erstwhile kidnapping plot. Harbin took Booth and Herold to another Confederate agent in the area, William Bryant, who supplied them with horses.

While Lincoln's funeral train was in New York City on April 24, Lieutenant Edward P. Doherty was dispatched from Washington at 2 p.m. with a detachment of 26 Union soldiers from the 16th New York Cavalry Regiment to capture Booth in Virginia. Accompanied by Lieutenant Colonel Everton Conger, an intelligence officer assigned by Lafayette Baker, the detachment steamed 70 miles (113 km) down the Potomac River on a boat, the *John S. Ide*, landing at Belle Plain, Virginia, at 10 p.m. The pursuers crossed the Rappahannock River and tracked Booth and Herold to Richard H. Garrett's farm, just south of Port Royal, Caroline County, Virginia. Booth and Herold had been led to the farm on April 24 by William S. Jett, a former private in the 9th Virginia Cavalry whom they had met before crossing the Rappahannock. The Garretts were unaware of Lincoln's assassination; Booth was introduced to them as

"James W. Boyd", a Confederate soldier who, they were told, had been wounded in the battle of Petersburg and was returning home.

Garrett's 11-year-old son, Richard, was an eyewitness. In later years, he became a Baptist minister and widely lectured on the events of Booth's demise at his family's farm. In 1921, Garrett's lecture was published in the *Confederate Veteran* as the "True Story of the Capture of John Wilkes Booth". According to his account, Booth and Herold arrived at the Garretts' farm, located on the road to Bowling Green, around 3 p.m. on Monday afternoon. Because Confederate mail delivery had ceased with the collapse of the Confederate government, he explained, the Garretts were unaware of Lincoln's assassination. After having dinner with the Garretts that evening, Booth learned of the surrender of Johnston's army. The last Confederate armed force of any size, its capitulation meant that the Civil War was unquestionably over and Booth's attempt to save the Confederacy by Lincoln's assassination had failed. The Garretts also finally learned of Lincoln's death and the substantial reward for Booth's capture. Booth, said Garrett, displayed no reaction, other than to ask if the family would turn in the fugitive should they have the opportunity. Still not aware of their guest's true identity, one of the older Garrett sons averred that they might, if only because they needed the money. The next day, Booth told the Garretts he intended to reach Mexico, drawing a route on a map of theirs. However, biographer Theodore Roscoe said of Garrett's account, "Almost nothing written or testified in respect to the doings of the fugitives at Garrett's farm can be taken at face value. Nobody knows exactly what Booth said to the Garretts, or they to him".

Death

Conger tracked down Jett and interrogated him, learning of Booth's location at the Garrett farm. Before dawn on April 26, the soldiers caught up with the fugitives, who were hiding in Garrett's tobacco barn. David Herold surrendered, but Booth refused Conger's demand to surrender, saying "I prefer to come out and fight"; the soldiers then set the barn on fire. As Booth moved about inside the blazing barn, Sergeant Boston Corbett shot him. According to Corbett's later account, he fired at Booth because the fugitive "raised his pistol to shoot" at them. Conger's report to Stanton, however, stated that Corbett shot Booth "without order, pretext or excuse", and recommended that Corbett be punished for disobeying orders to take Booth alive. Booth, fatally wounded in the neck, was dragged from the barn to the porch of Garrett's farmhouse, where he died three hours later, aged 26. The bullet had pierced three vertebrae and partially severed his spinal cord, paralyzing him. In his last dying moments, he

The porch of the Garrett farmhouse, where Booth died in 1865

reportedly whispered "tell my mother I died for my country". Asking that his hands be raised to his face so he could see them, Booth uttered his last words, "Useless, useless," and died as dawn was breaking.

In Booth's pockets were found a compass, a candle, pictures of five women, including his fiancée Lucy Hale, and his diary, where he had written of Lincoln's death, "Our country owed all her troubles to him, and God simply made me the instrument of his punishment."

Shortly after Booth's death, his brother Edwin wrote to his sister Asia, "Think no more of him as your brother; he is dead to us now, as he soon must be to all the world, but imagine the boy you loved to be in that better part of his spirit, in another world." Asia also had in her possession a sealed letter Booth had given her in January 1865 for safekeeping, only to be opened upon his death. In the letter, Booth had written:

> "I know how foolish I shall be deemed for undertaking such a step as this, where, on one side, I have many friends and everything to make me happy ... to give up all ... seems insane; but God is my judge. I love justice more than I do a country that disowns it, more than fame or wealth."

Booth's letter, seized along with other family papers at Asia's house by Federal troops and published by *The New York Times* while the manhunt was underway, explained his reasons for plotting against Lincoln. In it he said, "I have ever held the South was right. The very nomination of Abraham Lincoln, four years ago, spoke plainly war upon Southern rights and institutions." The institution of "African slavery", he had written, "is one of the greatest blessings that God has ever bestowed upon a favored nation" and Lincoln's policy was one of "total annihilation".

Aftermath

Booth's body was shrouded in a blanket and tied to the side of an old farm wagon for the trip back to Belle Plain. There, his corpse was taken aboard the ironclad USS *Montauk* and brought to the Washington Navy Yard for identification and an autopsy. The body was identified there as Booth's by more than ten people who knew him. Among the identifying features used to make sure that the man that was killed was Booth was a tattoo on his left hand with his initials J.W.B., and a distinct scar on the back of his neck. The third, fourth, and fifth vertebrae were removed during the autopsy to allow access to the bullet. These bones are still on display at the National Museum of Health and Medicine in Washington, D.C. The body was then buried in a storage room at the Old Penitentiary, later moved to a warehouse at the Washington Arsenal on October 1, 1867. In 1869, the remains were once again identified before being released to the Booth family, where they were buried in the family plot at Green Mount Cemetery in Baltimore, after a burial ceremony conducted by Fleming James,

The Historic Site marker on U.S. Route 301 near Port Royal, where the Garrett barn and farmhouse once stood in what is now the highway's median

minister of Christ Episcopal Church, in the presence of more than 40 people. By then, wrote scholar Russell Conwell after visiting homes in the vanquished former Confederate states, hatred of Lincoln still smoldered and "Photographs of Wilkes Booth, with the last words of great martyrs printed upon its borders ... adorn their drawing rooms".

Eight others implicated in Lincoln's assassination were tried by a military tribunal in Washington, D.C., and found guilty on June 30, 1865. Mary Surratt, Lewis Powell, David Herold, and George Atzerodt were hanged in the Old Arsenal Penitentiary on July 7, 1865. Samuel Mudd, Samuel Arnold, and Michael O'Laughlen were sentenced to life imprisonment at Fort Jefferson in Florida's Dry Tortugas; Edmund Spangler was given a six-year term in prison. O' Laughlen died in a yellow fever epidemic there in 1867. The others were eventually pardoned in February 1869 by President Andrew Johnson.

Forty years later, when the centenary of Lincoln's birth was celebrated in 1909, a border state official reflected on Booth's assassination of Lincoln, "Confederate veterans held public services and gave public expression to the sentiment, that 'had Lincoln lived' the days of reconstruction might have been softened and the era of good feeling ushered in earlier". A century later, Goodrich concluded in 2005, "For millions of people, particularly in the South, it would be decades before the impact of the Lincoln assassination began to release its terrible hold on their lives". The majority of Northerners viewed Booth as a madman or monster who murdered the savior of the Union, while in the South, many cursed Booth for bringing upon them the harsh revenge of an incensed North instead of the reconciliation promised by Lincoln.

Theories of Booth's escape

Main article: James William Boyd

In 1907, Finis L. Bates wrote *Escape and Suicide of John Wilkes Booth*, contending that a Booth look-alike was mistakenly killed at the Garrett farm while Booth eluded his pursuers. Booth, said Bates, assumed the pseudonym "John St. Helen" and settled on the Paluxy River near Glen Rose, Texas, and later moved to Granbury, Texas. After falling gravely ill and making a deathbed confession that he was the fugitive assassin, he recovered and fled, eventually committing suicide in 1903 in Enid, Oklahoma, under the alias "David E. George". By 1913, more than 70,000 copies of the book had been sold, and Bates exhibited St. Helen's mummified body in carnival sideshows.

The Booth Family gravesite, Green Mount Cemetery, where Booth is buried in an unmarked grave

In response, the Maryland Historical Society published an account in 1913 by then-Baltimore mayor William M. Pegram, who had viewed Booth's remains upon the casket's arrival at the Weaver funeral home in Baltimore on February 18, 1869, for burial at Green Mount Cemetery. Pegram, who had known Booth well as a young man, submitted a sworn statement that the body he had seen in 1869 was Booth's. Others positively identifying this body as Booth at the funeral home included Booth's mother, brother, and sister, along with his dentist and other Baltimore acquaintances. Earlier, *The New York Times* had published an account by their reporter in 1911 detailing the burial of Booth's body at the cemetery and those who were witnesses. The rumor periodically revived, as in the 1920s, when a corpse advertised as the "Man Who Shot Lincoln" was exhibited on a national tour by a carnival promoter. According to a 1938 article in the *Saturday Evening Post*, the exhibitor said he obtained St. Helen's corpse from Bates' widow.

The Lincoln Conspiracy, a book published in 1977, contended there was a government plot to conceal Booth's escape, reviving interest in the story and prompting the display of St. Helen's mummified body in Chicago that year. The book sold more than one million copies and was made into a feature film called *The Lincoln Conspiracy*, which was theatrically released in 1977. A 1998 book, *The Curse of Cain: The Untold Story of John Wilkes Booth*, contended that Booth had escaped, sought refuge in Japan and eventually returned to the United States. In 1994 two historians, together with several descendants, sought a court order for the exhumation of Booth's body at Green Mount Cemetery, which was, according to their lawyer, "intended to prove or disprove longstanding theories on Booth's escape" by conducting a photo-superimposition analysis. The application was blocked, however, by Baltimore Circuit Court Judge Joseph H. H. Kaplan, who cited, among other things, "the unreliability of petitioners' less-than-convincing escape/cover-up theory" as a major factor in his decision. The Maryland Court of Special Appeals upheld the ruling. No gravestone marks the precise location where Booth is buried in the family's gravesite. Author Francis Wilson, 11 years old at the time of Lincoln's assassination, wrote an epitaph of Booth in his 1929 book *John Wilkes Booth*: "In the terrible deed he committed, he was actuated by no thought of monetary gain, but by a self-sacrificing, albeit wholly fanatical devotion to a cause he thought supreme."

References

Bibliography

- Allen, Thomas B. (1992). *The Blue and the Gray*. Washington, D.C.: National Geographic Society. ISBN 0870448765.
- Balsiger, David and Sellier, Charles Jr. (1994). *The Lincoln Conspiracy*. Buccaneer. ISBN 1-56849-531-5.
- Bates, Finis L. (1907). *Escape and Suicide of John Wilkes Booth* [1]. Atlanta, Ga.: J. L. Nichols. LCCN 45-052628 [2].
- Bishop, Jim (1955). *The Day Lincoln Was Shot*. Harper & Row. LCCN 54-012170 [3].
- Clarke, Asia Booth (1996). Terry Alford. ed. *John Wilkes Booth: A Sister's Memoir*. Jackson, Miss.: University Press of Mississippi. ISBN 0-87805-883-4.
- Coates, Bill (August 22, 2006). "Tony Blair and John Wilkes Booth" [4]. *Madera Tribune*.
- Donald, David Herbert (1995). *Lincoln*. New York: Simon & Schuster. ISBN 0-684-80846-3.
- Freiberger, Edward (February 26, 1911). "Grave of Lincoln's Assassin Disclosed at Last" [5] (PDF). *The New York Times*.
- Garrett, Richard Baynham (October 1963). "A Chapter of Unwritten History: Richard Baynham Garrett's Account of the Flight and Death of John Wilkes Booth" [6]. In Fleet, Betsy. *The Virginia Magazine of History and Biography, Vol. 71, No. 4*. Virginia Historical Society.
- Goodrich, Thomas (2005). *The Darkest Dawn*. Bloomington, Ind.: Indiana University. ISBN 0-253-32599-4.
- Gorman, Francis J. (1995). "Exposing the myth that John Wilkes Booth escaped" [7]. Gorman and Williams.
- Hanchett, William (1986). *The Lincoln Murder Conspiracies* [8]. University of Illinois Press. ISBN 0252013611.
- Hansen, Peter A. (February 2009). "The funeral train, 1865". *Trains* (Kalmbach) **69** (2). ISSN 0041-0934 [9].
- Johnson, Byron B. (1914). *John Wilkes Booth and Jefferson Davis – a true story of their capture* [10]. Boston: The Lincoln & Smith Press.
- Johnston, Alva (February 19, 1928). "John Wilkes Booth on Tour". *Saturday Evening Post* **CCX**.
- Kauffman, Michael W. (2004). *American Brutus: John Wilkes Booth and the Lincoln Conspiracies*. New York: Random House. ISBN 037550785X.
- Kauffman, Michael W. (1978). "Fort Lesley McNair and the Lincoln Conspirators". *Lincoln Herald* **80**.
- Kauffman, Michael W. (May–June 1995). "Historians Oppose Opening of Booth Grave". *Civil War Times*.
- Kimmel, Stanley (1969). *The Mad Booths of Maryland*. New York: Dover. LCCN 69-019162 [11].

- Kunhardt, Dorothy and Philip, Jr. (1965). *Twenty Days*. North Hollywood, Calif.: Newcastle. LCCN 62-015660 [12].
- Kunhardt, Jr., Philip (1983). *A New Birth of Freedom*. Boston: Little, Brown. ISBN 0-316-50600-1.
- Kunhardt III, Philip B. (February 2009). "Lincoln's Contested Legacy". *Smithsonian* **39** (11).
- Lockwood, John (March 1, 2003). "Booth's oil-field venture goes bust". *The Washington Times*.
- Lorant, Stefan (1954). *The Life of Abraham Lincoln*. New American Library. LCCN 56-027706 [13].
- McCardell, Lee (December 27, 1931). "The body in John Wilkes Booth's grave". *The Baltimore Sun*.
- Mudd, Samuel A. (1906). Mudd, Nettie. ed. *The Life of Dr. Samuel A. Mudd* [14] (4th ed.). New York and Washington: Neale Publishing Company.
- "John Wilkes Booth's Escape Route" [15]. *Ford's Theatre, National Historic Site*. National Park Service. December 22, 2004. Archived from the original [16] on 2008-01-25. Retrieved 2007-10-15.
- Nottingham, Theodore J. (1998). *The Curse of Cain: The Untold Story of John Wilkes Booth*. Sovereign. ISBN 1-58006-021-8.
- Pegram, William M. (December 1913). "The body of John Wilkes Booth". *Journal* (Maryland Historical Society).
- Rhodehamel, John and Taper, Louise, ed (1997). *Right or Wrong, God Judge Me: The Writings of John Wilkes Booth*. Urbana, Ill.: University of Illinois. ISBN 0252023471.
- Schlichenmeyer, Terri (August 21, 2007). "Missing body parts of famous people" [17]. CNN.
- Sheads, Scott and Toomey, Daniel (1997). *Baltimore During the Civil War*. Linthicum, Md.: Toomey Press. ISBN 0-9612670-7-0.
- Smith, Gene (1992). *American Gothic: the story of America's legendary theatrical family, Junius, Edwin, and John Wilkes Booth*. New York: Simon & Schuster. ISBN 0-671-76713-5.
- Steers, Jr., Edward (2001). *Blood on the Moon: The Assassination of Abraham Lincoln*. University Press of Kentucky. ISBN 9780813122175.
- Stern, Philip Van Doren (1955). *The Man Who Killed Lincoln*. Garden City, NY: Dolphin. LCCN 99-215784 [18].
- "Dredging up the John Wilkes Booth body argument". *The Baltimore Sun*. December 13, 1977.
- "Harford expected to OK renovation of Booth home". *The Baltimore Sun*. September 8, 2008.
- Thomas, Benjamin P. (1952). *Abraham Lincoln, a Biography*. New York: Knopf. LCCN 52-006425 [19].
- "The murderer of Mr. Lincoln" [20] (PDF). *The New York Times*. April 21, 1865.
- "John Wilkes Booth's Last Days" [21] (PDF). *The New York Times*. July 30, 1896.
- "New Scrutiny on John Wilkes Booth" [22]. *The New York Times*. October 24, 1994.
- Toomey, Daniel Carroll. *The Civil War in Maryland*. Baltimore, Md.: Toomey Press. ISBN 0-9612670-0-3.
- Townsend, George Alfred (1865). *The Life, Crime and Capture of John Wilkes Booth* [23] (1977 ed.). New York: Dick and Fitzgerald. ISBN 978-0976480532.

- Ward, Geoffrey C. (1990). *The Civil War – an illustrated history*. New York: Alfred A. Knopf. ISBN 0-394-56285-2.
- Westwood, Philip (2002). "The Lincoln-Blair Affair" [24]. Genealogy Today.
- Wilson, Francis (1972). *John Wilkes Booth*. New York: Blom. LCCN 74-091588 [25].

Further reading

- Bak, Richard (1954). *The Day Lincoln Was Shot*. Dallas, Texas: Taylor. ISBN 0878332006.
- Goodrich, Thomas (2005). *The Darkest Dawn: Lincoln, Booth, and the Great American Tragedy*. Bloomington, Ind.: Indiana University. ISBN 0253345677.
- Reck, W. Emerson (1987). *A. Lincoln: His Last 24 Hours*. Jefferson, N.C.: McFarland. ISBN 0899502164.
- Swanson, James L. (2006). *Manhunt: The 12-Day Chase for Lincoln's Killer*. New York: William Morrow. ISBN 0060518499.
- Turner, Thomas R. (1999). *The Assassination of Abraham Lincoln*. Malabar, Fla.: Krieger. ISBN 1575240033.

For younger readers

- Giblin, James Cross (2005). *Good Brother, Bad Brother*. New York: Clarion. ISBN 0-618-09642-6.

External links

- Cervical (Neck) Vertebrae [26] preserved at National Museum of Health and Medicine
- Autopsy [27]
- Lieut. Doherty's report to the War Department on 29 April 1865, recounting Booth's capture [28]
- Booth: Escape and wanderings until final ending of the trail by suicide at Enid, Oklahoma, January 12, 1903 (1922) [29] Digitized by the University of Illinois at Urbana-Champaign Library
- The life, crime, and capture of John Wilkes Booth, with a full sketch of the conspiracy of which he was the leader, and the pursuit, trial and execution of his accomplices (1865) [30] Digitized by the University of Illinois at Urbana-Champaign Library.
- "John Wilkes Booth FBI file" [31]. Federal Bureau of Investigation. October 17, 2006. Archived from the original [32] on September 12, 2008. "These records contain correspondence dated 1922–1923 of William J. Burns, former Director of the Bureau of Investigation, concerning a theory that Booth lived many years after the assassination of President Lincoln."
- Geringer, Joseph (2008). "John Wilkes Booth: The Story of Abraham Lincoln's Murderer" [33]. truTV.
- Linder, Douglas (2002). "Last Diary Entry of John Wilkes Booth" [34]. University of Missouri–Kansas City.

- "Hunt for Abraham Lincoln's Assassin, John Wilkes Booth" [35]. *History.com*. A&E Television Networks. 2008.
- Encyclopedia of Oklahoma History and Culture - Booth Legend [36]
- John Wilkes Booth (I) [37] at Find a Grave
- John Wilkes Booth (II) [38] at Find a Grave

Two Ohio Presidents are Assassinated

Charles J. Guiteau

Charles Julius Guiteau	
Charles Julius Guiteau	
Born	September 8, 1841 Freeport, Illinois, U.S.
Died	June 30, 1882 (aged 40) Washington, D.C., U.S.
Charge(s)	assassination of a U.S. President
Penalty	Death by hanging
Status	Executed
Occupation	Lawyer
Spouse	Annie Bunn (divorced)
Children	none

Charles Julius Guiteau (September 8, 1841 – June 30, 1882) was an American lawyer who assassinated U.S. President James A. Garfield on July 2, 1881. He was executed by hanging.

Background

Guiteau was born in Freeport, Illinois, the fourth of six children of Luther Wilson Guiteau and Jane Howe. He moved with his family to Ulao, Wisconsin, (now Grafton, Wisconsin) in 1850 and lived there until 1855, when his mother died. Soon after, Guiteau and his father moved back to Freeport.[citation needed]

He inherited $1,000 from his grandfather (worth about $NaN in year–2011 dollars) as a young man and went to Ann Arbor, Michigan, in order to attend the University of Michigan. Due to inadequate academic preparation, he failed the entrance examinations. After some time trying to do remedial work in Latin and algebra at Ann Arbor High School, during which time he received numerous letters from his father haranguing him to do so, he quit and joined the utopian religious sect known as the Oneida Community, in Oneida, New York, with which Guiteau's father already had close affiliations. Despite the "group marriage" aspects of that sect, he was generally rejected during his five years there, and was nicknamed "Charles Gitout". He left the community twice. The first time he went to Hoboken, New Jersey, and attempted to start a newspaper based on Oneida religion, to be called "The Daily Theocrat". This failed and he returned to Oneida, only to leave again and file lawsuits against the community's founder, John Humphrey Noyes. Guiteau's father, embarrassed, wrote letters in support of Noyes, who had considered Guiteau irresponsible and insane.

Guiteau then obtained a law license in Chicago, based on an extremely casual bar exam. He used his money to start a law firm in Chicago based on ludicrously fraudulent recommendations from virtually every prominent American family of the day.[citation needed] He was not successful. He argued only one case in court, the bulk of his business being in bill collecting. Most of his cases resulted in enraged clients and judicial criticism.[citation needed]

He next turned to theology. He published a book on the subject called *The Truth* which was almost entirely plagiarized from the work of John Humphrey Noyes.[citation needed]

Guiteau's interest turned to politics. He wrote a speech in support of Ulysses S. Grant called "Grant vs. Hancock", which he revised to "Garfield vs. Hancock" after Garfield won the Republican nomination in the 1880 presidential campaign. Ultimately, he changed little more than the title (hence mixing up Garfield's achievements with those of Grant).[citation needed] The speech was delivered at most two times (and copies were passed out to members of the Republican National Committee at their summer 1880 meeting in New York), but Guiteau believed himself to be largely responsible for Garfield's victory. He insisted he should be awarded an ambassadorship for his vital assistance, first asking for Vienna, then deciding that he would rather be posted in Paris. His personal requests to the President and to cabinet members (as one of many job seekers who lined up every day) were continually rejected; on May 14, 1881, he was finally told personally never to return by Secretary of State James G. Blaine (Guiteau is actually believed to have encountered Blaine on more than one occasion).[citation needed]

Assassination of Garfield

Main article: James A. Garfield assassination

President James A. Garfield with Secretary of State James G. Blaine after being shot by Guiteau, as depicted in a period engraving from *Frank Leslie's Illustrated Newspaper*.

Guiteau then decided that God had commanded him to kill the ungrateful president. Borrowing fifteen dollars, he went out to purchase a revolver. He knew little about firearms, but did know that he would need a large caliber gun. He had to choose between a .442 Webley British Bulldog revolver with wooden grips and one with ivory grips. He wanted the one with the ivory handle because he wanted it to look good as a museum exhibit after the assassination, but he could not afford the extra dollar. (The revolver was recovered and even photographed by the Smithsonian in the early 20th century but has since been lost). He spent the next few weeks in target practice—the kick from the revolver almost knocked him over the first time—and stalking the president.

On one occasion, he trailed Garfield to the railway station as the president was seeing his wife off to a beach resort in Long Branch, New Jersey, but he decided to shoot him later, as Mrs. Garfield was in poor health and Guiteau did not want to upset her. On July 2, 1881, he lay in wait for the president at the (since demolished) Baltimore and Potomac Railroad Station, getting his shoes shined, pacing, and engaging a cab to take him to the jail later. As President Garfield entered the station, looking forward to a vacation with his wife in Long Branch, New Jersey, Guiteau stepped forward and shot Garfield twice from behind, the second shot piercing the first lumbar vertebra but missing the spinal cord. As he surrendered to authorities, Guiteau fired with the exulting words, repeated everywhere: "I am a Stalwart of the Stalwarts. .. Arthur is president now!!'" (*New York Herald*, July 3, 1881).

Contemporary illustration of Guiteau's pistol

After a long, painful battle with infections possibly brought on by his doctors' poking and probing the wound with unwashed hands and non-sterilized instruments, Garfield died on September 19, eleven weeks after being shot. Most modern physicians familiar with the case state that Garfield would have easily recovered from his wounds with sterile medical care, which was common in the United States 10 years later.

Trial and execution

Once President Garfield died, the government officially charged Guiteau with murder. The trial began on November 14, 1881, in Washington, D.C. The presiding judge in the case was Walter Smith Cox. Guiteau's court-appointed defense lawyers were Leigh Robinson and George Scoville, although Guiteau would insist on trying to represent himself during the entire trial. Wayne MacVeagh, the U.S. Attorney, served as the chief prosecutor. MacVeagh named five lawyers to the prosecution team: George Corkhill, Walter Davidge, John K. Porter, Elihu Root, and E.B. Smith.[citation needed]

1881 political cartoon showing Guiteau holding a gun and a note that says "*An office or your life!*" The caption for the cartoon reads "Model Office Seeker."

Guiteau's trial was one of the first high-profile cases in the United States where the insanity defense was considered. Guiteau vehemently insisted that while he had been legally insane at the time of the shooting, he was not really medically insane, which was one of the major causes of the rift between him and his defense lawyers and probably also a reason the jury assumed Guiteau was merely trying to deny responsibility for the murder of the president.[citation needed]

George Corkhill, who was the District of Columbia's district attorney and on the prosecuting team, summed up the prosecution's opinion of Guiteau's insanity defense in a pre-trial press statement that also mirrored public opinion on the issue. Corkhill stated;

> *He's no more insane than I am. There's nothing of the mad about Guiteau: he's a cool, calculating blackguard, a polished ruffian, who has gradually prepared himself to pose in this way before the world. He was a deadbeat, pure and simple. Finally, he got tired of the monotony of deadbeating. He wanted excitement of some other kind and notoriety, and he got it.*

—George Corkhill - District attorney for District of Columbia

Guiteau became something of a media darling during his entire trial for his bizarre behavior, including constantly cursing and badmouthing the judge, witnesses, and even his defense team, formatting his testimony in epic poems which he recited at length, and soliciting legal advice from random spectators in the audience via passed notes. He dictated an autobiography to the *New York Herald*, ending it with a personal ad for a nice Christian lady under thirty. He was blissfully oblivious to the American public's outrage and hatred of him, even after he was almost assassinated twice himself. He frequently smiled and waved at spectators and reporters in and out of the courtroom, seemingly happy to be the center of attention for once in his life. At one point, Guiteau argued before Judge Cox that President Garfield was killed not by the bullets but by medical malpractice ("The doctors killed Garfield, I just shot him"), which was more than a little true. But Guiteau's argument had no legal support. Throughout the trial and up until his execution, Guiteau was housed at St. Elizabeths Hospital in the southeastern quadrant of Washington, D.C. While in prison and awaiting execution, Guiteau wrote a defense of the assassination he had committed and an account of his own trial, which was published as *The Truth and the Removal* [1].

To the end, Guiteau was actively making plans to start a lecture tour after his perceived imminent release and to run for president himself in 1884, while at the same time continuing to delight in the media circus surrounding his trial. He was dismayed when the jury was unconvinced of his divine inspiration, convicting him of the murder. He was found guilty on January 25, 1882. After the guilty verdict was read, Guiteau stepped forward, despite his lawyers' efforts to tell him to be quiet, and yelled at the jury saying "You are all low, consummate jackasses!" plus a further stream of curses and obscenities before he was taken away by guards to his cell to await execution. Guiteau appealed his conviction, but his appeal was rejected, and he was hanged on June 30, 1882, in the District of Columbia. Of the four presidential assassins, Guiteau lived longer than any after his victim's death (nine months). While being led to his execution, Guiteau was said to have continued to smile and wave at spectators and reporters, happy to be at the center of attention to the very end. On the scaffold as a last request, he recited a poem he had written during his incarceration which he called "I am Going to the Lordy." [2] He had originally requested an orchestra to play as he sang his poem, but this request was denied.

Part of Guiteau's brain remains on display at the Mütter Museum in Philadelphia.[citation needed]

In popular culture

- Charlie Guiteau is a featured character in Stephen Sondheim's controversial musical, *Assassins*.
- Guiteau is mentioned in the song "Mr. Garfield" written by Ramblin' Jack Elliott and sung by Johnny Cash.[citation needed]

See also

- List of assassins
- Patronage
- List of people who died by hanging

External links

- History House [3]'s account of Guiteau's life and the assassination of Garfield, part 1 [4], 2 [5] and 3 [6].
- The Truth and the Removal [1].

Leon Czolgosz

Leon Czolgosz	
Photo from 1900, found among Czolgosz's effects.	
Born	Alpena, Michigan, USA
Died	October 29, 1901 (aged 28) Auburn, New York, USA
Charge(s)	First-degree murder
Penalty	Death
Status	Executed by electric chair
Occupation	Steel worker
Parents	Mary (Nowak) and Paul Czolgosz
Children	Nicole Uzieda and Ziz Pairrj

Leon Frank Czolgosz (Polish pronunciation: [ˈt͡sɔlɡɔʂ]; May 5, 1873 – October 29, 1901; also used surname "Nieman" and variations thereof) was the assassin of U.S. President William McKinley. In the last few years of his life, he claimed to have been heavily influenced by anarchists such as Emma Goldman and Alexander Berkman.

Early life

Czolgosz was born in Alpena, Michigan in 1873, one of eight children (six boys and two girls) of Mary (née Nowak) and Paul Czolgosz, Polish Catholic immigrants from Prussia. He was baptized in St. Albertus Catholic Church. His family moved to Detroit when he was five years old.

He left his family farm in Warrensville, Ohio, at the age of ten to work at the American Steel and Wire Company with two of his brothers. After the workers of his factory went on strike, he and his brothers were fired. Czolgosz then returned to the family farm in Warrensville. At the age of sixteen. he was sent to work in a glass factory in Natrona, Pennsylvania for two years before moving back home.

Interest in anarchism

Part of the Politics series on

Anarchism

Anarchism Portal
Politics portal

In 1898, after witnessing a series of similar strikes (many ending in violence), Czolgosz again returned home where he was constantly at odds with his stepmother and with his family's Roman Catholic beliefs. It was later recounted that through his life he had never shown any interest in friendship or romantic relationships, and was bullied throughout his childhood by peers. He became a recluse and spent much of his time alone reading Socialist and anarchist newspapers. He was impressed after hearing a speech by the political radical Emma Goldman, whom he met for the first time during one of her lectures in Cleveland in 1901. After the lecture Czolgosz approached the speakers' platform and asked for reading recommendations. A few days later he visited her home in Chicago and introduced himself as *Nieman*, but Goldman was on her way to the train station. He only had enough time to explain to her about his disappointment in Cleveland's socialists, and for Goldman to introduce him to her anarchist friends who were at the train station. She later wrote a piece in defense of Czolgosz.

Czolgosz was never known to be accepted into any anarchist group. Indeed, his fanaticism and comments about violence aroused anarchists' suspicions; some even thought he might have been a covert government agent.

The radical *Free Society* newspaper issued a warning pertaining to Czolgosz, reading:

> "The attention of the comrades is called to another spy. He is well dressed, of medium height, rather narrow shoulders, blond and about 25 years of age. Up to the present he has made his appearance in Chicago and Cleveland. In the former place he remained but a short time, while in Cleveland he disappeared when the comrades had confirmed themselves of his identity and were on the point of exposing him. His demeanor is of the usual sort, pretending to be greatly interested in the cause, asking for names or soliciting aid for acts of contemplated violence. If this same individual makes his appearance elsewhere the comrades are warned in advance, and can act accordingly."

Czolgosz's experiences had convinced him there was a great injustice in American society, an inequality which allowed the wealthy to enrich themselves by exploiting the poor. He concluded that the reason for this was the structure of government itself. Then he learned of a European crime which changed his life. On July 29, 1900, King Umberto I of Italy had been shot dead by anarchist Gaetano Bresci. Bresci told the press that he had decided to take matters into his own hands for the sake of the common man.

The assassination shocked and galvanized the American anarchist movement, and Czolgosz is thought to have consciously imitated Bresci. Joseph Petrosino's warnings were useless, because McKinley ignored them.

Assassination of President McKinley

Main article: Assassination of William McKinley

On August 31, 1901, Czolgosz moved to Buffalo, New York. There, he rented a room near the site of the Pan-American Exposition.

On September 6 he went to the exposition with a .32 caliber Iver-Johnson "Safety Automatic" revolver (serial #463344) he claimed he had purchased on September 2 for $4.50. With the gun wrapped in a handkerchief in his pocket, Czolgosz approached McKinley's procession, the President having been standing in a receiving line inside of the Temple of Music, greeting the public for 10 minutes. At 4:07 p.m. Czolgosz reached the front of the line. The President extended his hand; Czolgosz slapped it aside and shot McKinley in the abdomen twice at point blank range.

A sketch of Czolgosz shooting McKinley.

Members of the crowd immediately subdued Czolgosz, before the 4th Brigade, National Guard Signal Corps and police intervened, and beat him so severely it was initially thought he might not live to stand trial. Czolgosz was then briefly held in a cell at Buffalo's 13th Precinct house at 346 Austin Street until moved to the city's police headquarters downtown.

Trial and execution

On September 13, the day before McKinley succumbed to his wounds, Czolgosz was transferred from the police headquarters, since the headquarters were undergoing repairs, to the Erie County Women's Penitentiary. On the 16th he was taken to the Erie County Jail before being arraigned before County Judge Emery. After the arraignment, he was transferred to Auburn State Prison.

A grand jury indicted Czolgosz on September 16, who spoke freely with his guards, yet refused all interaction with Robert C. Titus and Lorin L. Lewis, the prominent judges-turned-attorneys assigned to defend him, and with the expert psychiatrist sent to test his sanity.

The district attorney at trial was Thomas Penney, assisted by a Mr. Haller, whose performance was described as "flawless". Although Czolgosz answered that he was pleading "Guilty", the presiding Judge Truman C. White overruled him and entered a "Not Guilty" plea on his behalf.

In the nine days from the death of President McKinley on September 14, to Czolgosz's trial on September 23, Czolgosz's lawyers had practically no time to prepare a defense since Czolgosz refused to speak to either one of them. As a result, Lorin Lewis argued at the trial that Czolgosz could not be found guilty for the murder of the president because he was insane at the time (similar to the defense that was used in the Charles J. Guiteau trial back in 1881, after the shooting of President James A. Garfield).

On September 23 and 24 prosecution testimony was presented, consisting of the doctors who treated McKinley and various eyewitnesses to the shooting. Loran Lewis did not call any defense witnesses. Czolgosz himself refused to testify on his own defense, nor did he ever speak at all in court. In his statement to the jury, Lewis noted Czolgosz's refusal to talk to his lawyers or cooperate with them, admitted his client's guilt, and said that "the only question that can be discussed or considered in this case is... whether that act was that of a sane person. If it was, then the defendant is guilty of the murder... If it was the act of an insane man, then he is not guilty of murder but should be acquitted of that charge and would then be confined in a lunatic asylum."

The prosecutor laid great stress on Czolgosz's anarchist affiliations and called upon the jury to heed the popular demand for a quick trial and execution. Since the defense had been unable to enter evidence that Czolgosz had been afflicted with any kind of temporary insanity, there could only be one verdict. Even if the jury believed the defense that Czolgosz was insane by claiming that no sane man would have shot and killed the president in such a public and blatant manner in which he knew he would be caught, there was still the legal definition of insanity to be overcome. Under New York law, Czolgosz was legally insane only if he was unable to understand what he was doing.

At Thomas Penney's request, Judge White closed the trial with instructions to the jury that supported the prosecution's argument that (a): Czolgosz was not insane, and that (b): he knew clearly what he was doing. After this, any chance that remained of acquitting Czolgosz on the basis of insanity was gone, since the defense offered no evidence that he couldn't understand the wrongness of his crime.

Czolgosz was convicted on September 24, 1901 after the jury deliberated for only one hour. On September 26, the jury recommended the death penalty. Upon returning to Auburn Prison, Czolgosz asked the warden if this meant he would be transferred to Sing Sing to be electrocuted, and seemed surprised to learn that Auburn had its own electric chair.

Czolgosz was electrocuted by three jolts, each of 1800 volts, in Auburn Prison on October 29, 1901. His brother, Waldek, and his brother-in-law, Frank Bandowski, were in attendance. When Waldek asked the Warden for his brother's body to be taken for proper burial, he was informed that he "would never be able to take it away" and that crowds of people would mob him.

His last words were "I killed the President because he was the enemy of the good people – the good working people. I am not sorry for my crime." As the prison guards strapped him into the chair, however, he did say through clenched teeth, "I am sorry I could not see my father." His brain was autopsied by Edward Anthony Spitzka.

Czolgosz's was autopsied by John T. Gerin. The body was buried on prison grounds following the autopsy. Prison authorities originally planned to inter the body with quicklime to hasten its decomposition, however they became dissatisfied with this option after testing quicklime on a sample of meat. After determining that they were not legally limited to the use of quicklime for the process, sulfuric acid was poured into Czolgosz's coffin so that his body would be completely disfigured. The warden estimated the acid caused the body to disintegrate within twelve hours.

Czolgosz's letters and clothes were burned, although in the case of letters the names of those who had sent threatening or sympathetic correspondence were recorded for future reference.

Legacy

Emma Goldman was arrested on suspicion of being involved in the assassination, but was released, due to insufficient evidence. She later incurred a great deal of negative publicity when she published "The Tragedy at Buffalo". In the article, she compared Czolgosz to Marcus Junius Brutus, the killer of Julius Caesar, and called McKinley the "president of the money kings and trust magnates." Other anarchists and radicals were unwilling to support Goldman's effort to aid Czolgosz, believing that he had harmed the movement.

The scene of the crime, the Temple of Music, was demolished in November 1901, along with the rest of the Exposition grounds. A stone marker in the middle of Fordham Drive, a residential street in Buffalo, marks the approximate spot (42°56.321′N 78°52.416′W) where the shooting occurred .

Czolgosz's revolver is on display in the Pan-American Exposition exhibit at the Buffalo and Erie County Historical Society in Buffalo. In 1921 Lloyd Vernon Briggs, Director of the Massachusetts Department for Mental Hygiene, reviewed the Czolgosz case and the cases of Clarence Richeson and Bertram G. Spencer. Contrary to views almost universally expressed at the time of the assassination, Briggs concluded that Czolgosz was "a diseased man, a man who had been suffering from some form of mental disease for years. He was not medically responsible and in the light of present-day psychiatry and of modern surgical procedure, there is a great question whether he was even legally responsible for the death of our President."

Czolgosz in film and popular culture

- The story of McKinley's assassination appears in a traditional folk song, known variously as "The White House Blues," "Zolgotz" (a corruption of the assassin's name), and "McKinley's Rag". Both Bascom Lamar Lunsford and Alan Lomax collected the song for the Library of Congress, the former on the record "Songs and Ballads of American History and of the Assassination of Presidents." It dates to at least 1923 and its original author is unknown.
- Czolgosz's story was the fictionalized theme of the play *Americans*, by Eric Schlosser.
- Czolgosz's story, along with those of eight other presidential assassins and would-be assassins, was the basis of Sondheim's and Weidman's Broadway musical *Assassins*. His story is told in the song *The Ballad of Czolgosz*.
- Czolgosz's activities on the day of the assassination are depicted in Brian Josepher's fictionalized chronicle of the 20th century, *What the Psychic Saw*.
- Czolgosz's execution by electrocution was recreated on film by Thomas Edison.
- Czolgosz is the escaped soul in "Leon", episode six of the first season of Reaper. He is played by Patton Oswalt.
- In Eleanor Updale's "Montmorency's Revenge", Czolgosz and his assassination of McKinley appear as a plot point in the second half of the novel.
- Czolgosz's story is the subject of John Smolens's novel "The Anarchist" (Three Rivers, December 2009).
- Czolgosz appears in the initial pages of Henry Miller's Tropic of Capricorn: "*I would have been better if, like the mad Czolgosz, I had shot some good President McKinley, some gentle, insignificant soul like that who never done anyone the least harm*".

The McKinley Monument before Buffalo's City Hall

Gallery

First photograph of Czolgosz in jail.

Police mug shot of Leon Czolgosz #757.

Czolgosz's prisoner card at Auburn #A2323.

Paul Czolgosz, Leon's father.

Jacob Czolgosz, Leon's brother.

See also

- Anarchism and violence
- Propaganda of the deed
- Assassination
- List of assassins

External links

- Film [1]: Reenactment of the execution of Leon Czolgosz in the electric chair, early film from 1901, Library of Congress archives (.rm format; offline viewable)
- PBS biography of Czolgosz [2]
- Leon Frank Czolgosz [3] at Find A Grave
- Stone marker at assassination site [4]

The Kennedy Brothers

Lee Harvey Oswald

Lee Harvey Oswald	
	Lee Harvey Oswald in Minsk, 1959
Born	October 18, 1939 New Orleans, Louisiana, U.S.
Died	November 24, 1963 (aged 24) Dallas, Texas, U.S.
Cause of death	Murdered by Jack Ruby
Nationality	American
Other names	**Alek J. Hidell** **O. H. Lee**
Spouse	Marina Prusakova (m. 1961)
	**Signature**

Lee Harvey Oswald

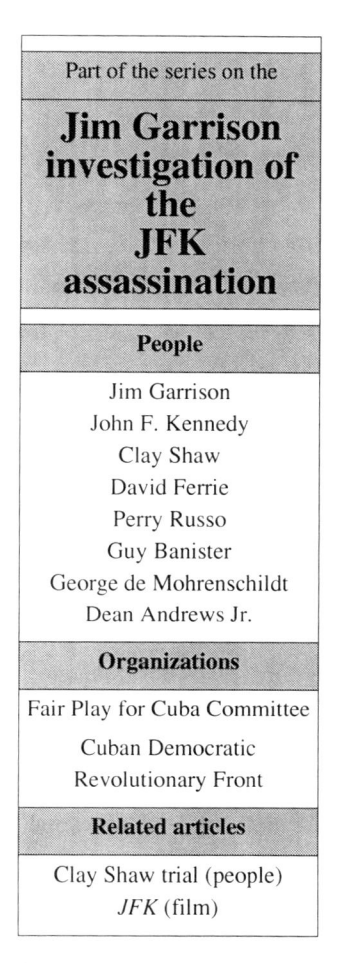

> **Part of the series on the**
>
> **Jim Garrison investigation of the JFK assassination**
>
> **People**
>
> Jim Garrison
> John F. Kennedy
> Clay Shaw
> David Ferrie
> Perry Russo
> Guy Banister
> George de Mohrenschildt
> Dean Andrews Jr.
>
> **Organizations**
>
> Fair Play for Cuba Committee
> Cuban Democratic Revolutionary Front
>
> **Related articles**
>
> Clay Shaw trial (people)
> *JFK* (film)

Lee Harvey Oswald (October 18, 1939 – November 24, 1963) was, according to four government investigations, the assassin of President of the United States John F. Kennedy, who was fatally shot in Dallas, Texas on November 22, 1963.

A former U.S. Marine who had briefly defected to the Soviet Union, Oswald was initially arrested for the murder of police officer J. D. Tippit, who had been shot dead on a Dallas street shortly after Kennedy was killed. Soon suspected in the assassination of Kennedy as well, Oswald denied involvement in either killing. Two days later, while being transferred from police headquarters to the county jail, Oswald was mortally wounded by nightclub owner Jack Ruby in full view of television cameras broadcasting live.

In 1964, the Warren Commission concluded that Oswald acted alone in assassinating Kennedy, a conclusion also reached by prior investigations carried out by the FBI and Dallas Police.

Biography

Childhood

Oswald was born in New Orleans on October 18, 1939, born to Robert Edward Lee Oswald, Sr. (New Orleans, Louisiana, March 4, 1896 – New Orleans, August 19, 1939) and Marguerite Frances Claverie (New Orleans, Louisiana, July 19, 1907 – Fort Worth, Texas, January 17, 1981). Oswald had two older siblings – brother Robert Edward Lee Oswald, Jr. and half-brother John Edward Pic.

Oswald's father died prior to Oswald's birth, and Marguerite raised her sons alone. When Oswald was two, his mother placed her sons at the Bethlehem Children's Home orphanage in New Orleans for thirteen months, as she was unable to support them.[citation needed] On May 7, 1945, his mother married Edwin Adolph Ekdahl (1888–1965) in Fort Worth, Texas; he engaged in numerous extra-marital affairs and filed for divorce in 1948.[citation needed]

As a child, Oswald had been withdrawn and temperamental. In August 1952, while living with half-brother John Pic, at the time a U.S. Coast Guardsman stationed in New York City, Oswald and Marguerite were asked to leave after Oswald allegedly threatened Pic's wife with a knife and struck their mother, Marguerite.

Charges of truancy, in the Bronx (NYC), had led to psychiatric assessment at a juvenile reformatory, the psychiatrist describing Oswald's "vivid fantasy life, turning around the topics of omnipotence and power, through which he tries to compensate for his present shortcomings and frustrations." Finding a "personality pattern disturbance with schizoid features and passive-aggressive tendencies," the psychiatrist recommended continued treatment. However, in January 1954, Oswald's mother Marguerite returned with him to New Orleans. At the time, there was a question pending before a New York judge as to whether Oswald should be removed from the care of his mother to finish his schooling, although his behavior appeared to improve during his last months in New York.

In New Orleans, in October 1955, Oswald left the 10th grade after one month. He worked as an office clerk or messenger around New Orleans, rather than attend school. Planning for his enlistment, the family returned to Fort Worth in July 1956, and he re-enrolled in 10th grade for the September session, but quit in October to join the Marines *(see below)*; he never received a high school diploma. By the of age 17, he had resided at 22 different locations and attended 12 different schools.

Though he had trouble spelling and writing coherently he read voraciously, and by age 15 claimed to be a Marxist, writing in his diary, "I was looking for a key to my environment, and then I discovered socialist literature. I had to dig for my books in the back dusty shelves of libraries." At 16 he wrote to the Socialist Party of America for information on their Young People's Socialist League, saying he had been studying socialist principles for "well over fifteen months." (However, Edward Voebel, "whom the Warren Commission had established was Oswald's closest friend during his teenage years in New Orleans...said that reports that Oswald was alreadyWikipedia:Manual_of_Style_(dates_and_numbers)#Chronological_items 'studying

Communism' were a 'lot of baloney.' " Voebel said that "Oswald commonly read 'paperback trash.' ")

Marine Corps

Oswald enlisted in the United States Marine Corps on October 24, 1956, just after his seventeenth birthday. He idolized his older brother Robert, and woreWikipedia:Manual_of_Style_(dates_and_numbers)#Chronological_items Robert's Marines ring. Enlistment may also have been an escape from Oswald's overbearing mother.

Oswald's primary training was as a radar operator, a position requiring a security clearance. A May 1957 document states that he was "granted final clearance to handle classified matter up to and including CONFIDENTIAL after careful check of local records had disclosed no derogatory data." In the Aircraft Control and Warning Operator Course he finished seventh in a class of thirty. The course "...included instruction in aircraft surveillance and the use of radar." He was assigned first to Marine Corps Air Station El Toro in July 1957, then to Naval Air Facility Atsugi in Japan in September as part of Marine Air Control Squadron 1. (Atsugi was a base for CIA U-2 spy planes flying over the Soviet Union, and Oswald may have subsequently passed information on this program to the Soviets.)

Like all Marines, Oswald was trained and tested in riflery, scoring 212 in December 1956 (slightly above the minimum for qualification as a *sharpshooter*) but in May 1959 scoring only 191 (barely earning the lower designation of *marksman*).

Oswald was court-martialed after accidentally shooting himself in the elbow with an unauthorized handgun, then court-martialed again for fighting with a sergeant he thought responsible for his punishment in the shooting matter. He was demoted from private first class to private and briefly imprisoned. He was later punished for a third incident: while on nighttime sentry duty in the Philippines, he inexplicably fired his rifle into the jungle.

Slightly built, Oswald was nicknamed *Ozzie Rabbit* after the cartoon character, or sometimes *Oswaldskovich* because of his pro-Soviet sentiments. In December 1958 he transferred back to El Toro, where his unit's function "...was to serveil [sic] for aircraft, but basically to train both enlisted men and officers for later assignment overseas." An officer there termed Oswald a "very competent" crew chief.

Oswald subscribedWikipedia:Manual_of_Style_(dates_and_numbers)#Chronological_items to the Communist newspaper *Daily Worker* and claimedWikipedia:Manual_of_Style_(dates_and_numbers)#Chronological_items to have taught himself rudimentary Russian, but in February 1959, he rated "poor" on a Marine proficiency exam in written and spoken Russian.

Defection to the Soviet Union

In October 1959, just before turning 20, Oswald traveled to the Soviet Union, the trip planned well in advance. Along with his self-taught Russian, he had saved $1,500 of his Marine Corps salary, got a hardship discharge (claiming his mother needed care) obtained a passport, and submitted several fictional applications to foreign universities in order to obtain a student visa.Wikipedia:Please clarify

Oswald spent two days with his mother in Fort Worth, then embarked by ship from New Orleans on September 20 to Le Havre, France, then immediately proceeded to England. Arriving in Southampton on October 9, he told officials he had $700 and planned to remain in the United Kingdom for one week before proceeding to a school in Switzerland. But on the same day, he flew to Helsinki, where he was issued a Soviet visa on October 14. Oswald left Helsinki by train on the following day, crossed the Soviet border at Vainikkala, and arrived in Moscow on October 16.

Almost immediately, Oswald told his Intourist guide of his desire to become a Soviet citizen, but was told on October 21 that his application had been refused. Oswald then inflicted a minor but bloody wound to his left wrist in his hotel room bathtub, after which the Soviets put him under psychiatric observation at a hospital.

On October 31 Oswald appeared at the United States embassy in Moscow, declaring a desire to renounce his U.S. citizenship. John McVickar, an official at the Moscow embassy, felt that Oswald, "...was following a pattern of behavior in which he had been tutored by [a] person or persons unknown...seemed to be using words which he had learned but did not fully understand...in short, it seemed to me that there was a possibility that he had been in contact with others before or during his Marine Corps tour who had guided him and encouraged him in his actions." He told Soviet officialsWikipedia:Manual_of_Style_(dates_and_numbers)#Chronological_items "...that he had been a radar operator in the Marine Corps and that he...would make known to them such information concerning the Marine Corps and his speciality as he possessed. He intimated that he might know something of special interest." (Such statements led to Oswald's *hardship/honorable* military discharge being changed to *undesirable*.)

Though Oswald had wanted to attend Moscow University, he was sent to Minsk to work as a lathe operator at the Gorizont (Horizon) Electronics Factory, a facility producing radios, televisions, and military and space electronics. He also received a subsidized,Wikipedia:Please clarify fully furnished studio apartment in a prestigious building and an additional supplement to his factory pay—all in all an idyllic existence by Soviet working-class standards, though, he was under constant surveillance.

Marina Prusakova, Minsk 1959

But Oswald grew bored in Minsk. He wrote in his diary in January 1961: "I am starting to reconsider my desire about staying. The work is drab, the

money I get has nowhere to be spent. No nightclubs or bowling alleys, no places of recreation except the trade union dances. I have had enough." Shortly afterwards, Oswald (who had never formally renounced his U.S. citizenship) wrote to the U.S. Embassy in Moscow requesting return of his American passport, and proposing to return to the U.S. if any charges against him would be dropped. (In 1964, Oswald's mother released an audio album, *The Oswald Case: Mrs. Marguerite Oswald Reads Lee Harvey Oswald's Letters from Russia,* on which she also comments on his letters.)

In March Oswald met Marina Prusakova, a 19-year-old pharmacology student; they married less than six weeks later. On July 11 Oswald and Marina applied at the U.S. Embassy in Moscow for documents enabling her to immigrate to the U.S. Their first child, June, was born on February 15, 1962, and on June 1 the family left for the United States, where they received a measure of attention in the press.

Dallas

The Oswalds now settled in the Dallas/Fort Worth area, where his mother and brother Robert lived, and Oswald began a memoir on Soviet life. Though he eventually gave up the project, his search for literary feedback put him in touch with anti-Communist Russian émigrés in the area. While merely tolerating the belligerent and arrogant Oswald, they sympathized with Marina, partly because she spoke no English—Oswald refused to teach her, saying he didn't want to forget Russian—and because Oswald had begun to beat her.

Although the Russian émigrés eventually abandoned Marina when she made no sign of leaving Oswald, Oswald found an unlikely friend in George de Mohrenschildt, a well-educated petroleum geologist. (A native Russian-speaker himself, de Mohrenschildt wrote that Oswald spoke Russian "very well, with only a little accent.") Marina meanwhile befriended Ruth Paine, who was trying to learn Russian, and her husband Michael.

In July 1962, Oswald was hired by Dallas' Leslie Welding Company; he disliked the work and quit after three months. In October he was hired by the graphic-arts firm of Jaggars-Chiles-Stovall as a photoprint trainee, but his inefficiency and rudeness were such that fights threatened to break out, and he was seen reading a Russian publication, *Krokodil.* He was fired during the first week of April 1963. (He may have used equipment at the firm to forge identification documents, including some in the name of an alias, *Alek James Hidell.*)

Attempt on life of General Walker

The Warren Commission concluded that on April 10, 1963, Oswald attempted to kill retired U.S. Major General Edwin Walker, an outspoken anti-communist, segregationist, and member of the John Birch Society who had been relieved of his command in 1962 for distributing right-wing literature to subordinates. His actions in opposition to racial integration at the University of Mississippi led to his arrest on insurrection, seditious conspiracy, and other charges, but a grand jury refused to indict him. Oswald considered Walker the leader of a "fascist organization."

In March 1963, Oswald purchased a 6.5 mm caliber Carcano rifle (commonly but improperly called Mannlicher-Carcano) by mail, using the alias *A. Hidell.* as well as a revolver by the same method.

The Warren Commission concluded that Oswald fired at Walker through a window, from less than 100 feet (30 m) away, as Walker sat at a desk in his home; the bullet struck the windowframe and Walker's only injury was bullet fragments to the forearm. Oswald returned home and told Marina what he had done.[citation needed] (The United States House Select Committee on Assassinations stated that the "evidence strongly suggested" that Oswald did the shooting.)

At the time, Dallas police had no suspects in the shooting, but Oswald's involvement was suspected within hours of his arrest following the Kennedy assassination. (A note Oswald left for Marina on the night of the attempt, telling her what to do if he did not return, was not found until early December 1963.) The Walker bullet was too damaged to run conclusive ballistics studies on it, but neutron activation tests later showed that it was "extremely likely" that it was made by the same manufacturer and for the same rifle make as the two bullets which later struck Kennedy.

New Orleans

Oswald returned to New Orleans on April 25; Marina joined him somewhat later.Wikipedia:Manual_of_Style_(dates_and_numbers)#Chronological_items In May he was hired by the Reily Coffee Company as a machinery greaser, but was fired in July for malingering.Wikipedia:Please clarify

On May 26 Oswald wrote to the New York City headquarters of the pro-Castro Fair Play for Cuba Committee, proposing to rent "...a small office at my own expense for the purpose of forming a FPCC branch here in New Orleans." (Oswald also referred to a having a public brawl with a Cuban refugee,

Oswald rented an apartment in this building in Uptown New Orleans c. May-September 1963

although no such fight is known to have occurred until two weeks later.) The FPCC Chairman rejected the proposal, commenting later on its suspicious nature.[citation needed]

According to Carlos Bringuier, on August 5 and 6 Oswald visited Bringuie, at the time the New Orleans delegate for the anti-Castro Cuban Student Directorate. Bringuier told the Warren Commission he believedWikipedia:Manual_of_Style_(dates_and_numbers)#Chronological_items

Oswald's visits were an attempt by Oswald to infiltrate his anti-Castro group. On August 9 Bringuier confronted Oswald as Oswald distributed pro-Castro fliers in downtown New Orleans. A scuffle led to the arrest of Oswald, Bringuier, and two friends of Bringuier's.

The incident received mediaWikipedia:Avoid weasel words attention which included an interview of Oswald.Wikipedia:Please clarify[citation needed] He was also filmed passing out fliers in front of the International Trade Mart with two hired helpers. But his political work in New Orleans came to an end after a radio debate between Bringuier and Oswald, during which Oswald was confronted about his past in the Soviet Union and his activities in New Orleans.Wikipedia:Please clarify

Oswald passing out "Fair Play for Cuba" leaflets in New Orleans, August, 1963.

Oswald's mid-1963 New Orleans activities were later investigated by New Orleans District Attorney Jim Garrison as part of his prosecution of Clay Shaw in 1969. Garrison was particularly interested in David Ferrie's possible connections to Oswald, which Ferrie himself denied; Ferrie died before being brought to trial. In 1993, the PBS television program *Frontline* obtained a photograph, taken eight years before the assassination, showing Oswald and Ferrie at a cookout with other Civil Air Patrol cadets.Wikipedia:Please clarify

Ron LewisWikipedia:Avoid weasel wordsWikipedia:Please clarify claimed that he briefly met David Ferrie and Guy Banister, and could substantiate certain claims made by Garrison,Wikipedia:Please clarify but decided not to risk personal danger testifying in the Shaw trial.Wikipedia:Please clarify[citation needed]

Further information: David Ferrie

Further information: Trial of Clay Shaw

Mexico

Marina returned to Dallas in late September 1963, but Oswald stayed in New Orleans at least two more days to collect a $33 unemployment check. It is uncertain when he left New Orleans: he is next known to have boarded a bus in Houston—bound for the Mexican border rather than Dallas, and telling other passengers he planned to travel to Cuba via Mexico. In Mexico City he applied for a transit visa at the Cuban Embassy, claiming he wanted to visit Cuba on his way back to the Soviet Union. Cuban officials insisted Oswald would need Soviet approval, but he was unable to get prompt co-operation from that embassy.

After five days of shuttling between consulates, a heated argument with the Cuban consul, impassioned pleas to KGB agents, and at least some CIA scrutiny, Oswald was told by the Cuban consul that he was disinclined to approve the visa, saying "a person like [Oswald] in place of aiding the Cuban Revolution, was doing it harm." Nonetheless, on October 18 the Cuban embassy indeed approved the visa, but Oswald did not in fact embark for Cuba.[*citation needed*] (Eleven days before the assassination of Kennedy, Oswald wrote to the Soviet embassy in Washington, D.C., saying, "Had I been able to reach the Soviet Embassy in Havana as planned, the embassy there would have had time to complete our business.")Wikipedia:Please clarify

Return to Dallas

Instead, on October 3 Oswald left by bus for Dallas, where on October 16 he began a job at the Texas School Book Depository. During the week he stayed in a Dallas rooming house (under the name *O.H. Lee*), but he spent weekends with Marina at the Paine home in Irving. On October 20 the Oswalds' second daughter was born. FBI agents twice visited the Paine home in early November, when Oswald was not present, looking for information on Marina, whom they suspected of being a Soviet agent. Oswald visited the Dallas FBI office about 7 to 10 days before the assassination, asking to see Special Agent James Hosty; told Hosty was unavailable, Oswald left a note that, according to the receptionist, read: "Let this be a warning. I will blow up the FBI and the Dallas Police Department if you don't stop bothering my wife. Signed - Lee Harvey Oswald."

In the days before Kennedy's arrival, several newspapers described the route of the presidential motorcade as passing the Book Depository. On November 21 Oswald asked a co-worker for a ride to Irving, saying he had to pick up some curtain rods. The next morning he returned to Dallas with Frazier; he left behind $170 and his wedding ring, but took with him a long paper bag. He was seen by a co-worker on the sixth floor of the depository about 30 minutes before the assassination.

Shootings of Kennedy and Tippit

Main article: John F. Kennedy assassination

Further information: Lone gunman theory

According to government investigations (including that of the Warren Commission) as Kennedy's motorcade passed through Dallas's Dealey Plaza about 12:30 p.m. on November 22, Oswald fired from a window on the sixth floor of the book depository, killing the President and seriously wounding Texas Governor John Connally. Bystander James Tague received a minor facial injury.

According to the Warren Commission, immediately after firing Oswald hid the rifle behind some boxes and descended the rear stairwell. About ninety seconds after the shooting, in the second-floor lunchroom he encountered a police officer accompanied by Oswald's supervisor; the officer let Oswald pass after the supervisor identified him as an employee. (According to the officer, Oswald was drinking a soda and did not appear to be nervous or out of breath.) Oswald crossed to the front staircase, and left the building just before police sealed it off. The supervisor later pointed out to officers that Oswald was the only employee to absent himself after the assassination.

Lee Harvey Oswald

At about 12:40 p.m. Oswald boarded a city bus but (probably due to heavy traffic) he requested a transfer from the driver and got off two blocks later. He took a taxicab to his rooming house, which he entered about 1:00 p.m., "walking pretty fast" according to his housekeeper. He soon left wearing a jacket, and was last seen by the housekeeper by the stop for a bus route heading back to downtown Dallas.

About four-fifths of a mile (1.3 km) away, Patrolman J. D. Tippit pulled alongside Oswald on a residential street and spoke to him through a window. At approximately 1:11–1:14 p.m., Tippit exited his car and was immediately struck and killed by four shots. Numerous witnesses heard the shots and saw a man flee the scene holding a revolver. Four cartridge cases found at the scene were identified by expert witnesses before the Warren Commission and the House Select Committee as having been fired from the revolver later found in Oswald's possession, to the exclusion of all other weapons.

Oswald's seat in the Texas Theater

Capture

Minutes later, Oswald was seen "ducking into" the entrance alcove of a shoe store, apparently avoiding passing police cars. Soon after, the store's manager saw Oswald slip into the nearby Texas Theater without paying. He alerted the theater's ticket clerk, who telephoned police.

As police arrived, the house lights were brought up as the store manager pointed out Oswald sitting near the rear. Oswald appeared to surrender (saying, "Well, it is all over now") but then struck an officer; he was disarmed after a struggle. As he was led from the theater, Oswald shouted he was a victim of police brutality.

Oswald being led from the Texas Theater after his arrest inside

At about 2 p.m., Oswald arrived at the Police Department building, where he was questioned by Detective Jim Leavelle in the shooting of Officer Tippit. When Captain J. W. Fritz heard Oswald's name, he recognized it as that of the Book Depository employee who was reported missing and was already a suspect in the assassination. Oswald was bookedWikipedia:Manual_of_Style_(dates_and_numbers)#Chronological_items for both murders, and by the end of the night he had been arraigned as well.

Soon after his capture Oswald encountered reporters in a hallway, declaring "I didn't shoot anyone" and "They're taking me in because of the fact I lived in the Soviet Union. I'm just a patsy!" Later, at an arranged press meeting, a reporter asked, "Did you kill the President?" and Oswald, who by that time had been advised of the charge of murdering Tippit, but not yet arraigned in Kennedy's death, answered "No, I have not been charged with that. In fact, nobody has said that to me yet. The first thing I heard about it was when the newspaper reporters in the hall asked me that question." As he was led from the room, "What did you do in Russia?" was called out, and "How did you hurt your eye?"; Oswald answered, "A policeman hit me."

Police interrogation

Oswald was interrogated several times during his two days at Dallas Police Headquarters. He denied killing Kennedy and Tippit, denied owning a rifle, said two photographs of him holding a rifle and a pistol were fakes, denied telling his co-worker he wanted a ride to Irving to get curtain rods for his apartment, and denied carrying a long heavy package to work the morning of the assassination. The Warren Commission also noted that Oswald denied knowing an *A. J. Hidell,* and when shown a forged Selective Service card bearing that name in his possession when arrested, refused to answer any questions concerning it, saying "...you have the card yourself and you know as much about it as I do." The Warren Commission noted that this "spurious" card bore the name of *Alek James Hidell.*

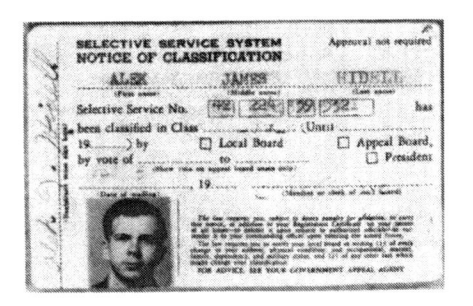

Fake selective service (draft) card in the name of *Alek James Hidell,* found on Oswald when arrested. *A.Hidell* was the name used on both envelope and order slip to buy the murder weapon (see CE 773), and *A. J. Hidell* was the alternate name on the post office box rented by Oswald, to which the weapon was sent

During his first interrogation on Friday, November 22, Oswald was asked to account for himself at the time the President was shot. Oswald said he ate lunch in the Depository's first-floor lunchroom, then went to the second floor for a Coca-Cola, where he encountered the policeman. During his last interrogation on November 24, Oswald was asked again where he was at the time of the shooting; he said he was working on an upper floor when it occurred, then went downstairs where he encountered the officer.

Oswald asked for legal representation several times while being interrogated, as well as in encounters with reporters. But when representatives of the Dallas Bar Association met with him in his cell on Saturday, he declined their services, saying he wanted to be represented by John Abt, chief counsel to the Communist Party USA, or by lawyers associated with the American Civil Liberties Union. Both

Oswald and Ruth Paine tried to reach Abt by telephone several times Saturday and Sunday, but Abt was away for the weekend. Oswald also declined his brother Robert's offer on Saturday to obtain a local attorney.

Death

See also: Jack Ruby

On Sunday, November 24 Oswald was being led through the basement of Dallas Police Headquarters preparatory to his transfer to the county jail when, at 11:21 a.m., Dallas nightclub operator Jack Ruby stepped from the crowd and shot Oswald in the abdomen. Oswald died at 1:07 p.m. at Parkland Memorial Hospital—the same hospital where Kennedy had died two days earlier.

A network television camera, there to cover the transfer, was broadcasting live at the time, and millions thereby witnessed the shooting as it happened. The event was also captured in a well-known photograph *(see right)*. Ruby later said he had been distraught over Kennedy's death, though other motives have been hypothesized.

After autopsy Oswald was buried in Fort Worth's Rose Hill Memorial Burial Park. A marker inscribed simply *Oswald* replaces the stolen original tombstone, which gave Oswald's full name and birth–death dates.

Official Investigations

Warren Commission

The Warren Commission, created by President Lyndon B. Johnson to investigate the assassination, concluded that Oswald acted alone in assassinating Kennedy (this view is known as the lone gunman theory). The Commission could not ascribe any one motive or group of motives to Oswald's actions:

> It is apparent, however, that Oswald was moved by an overriding hostility to his environment. He does not appear to have been able to establish meaningful relationships with other people. He was perpetually discontented with the world around him. Long before the assassination he expressed his hatred for American society and acted in protest against it. Oswald's search for what he conceived to be the perfect society was doomed from the start. He sought for himself a place in history — a role as the "great man" who would be recognized as having been in advance of his times. His commitment to Marxism and communism appears to have been another important factor in his motivation. He also had demonstrated a capacity to act decisively and without regard to the consequences when such action would further his aims of the moment. Out of these and the many other factors which may have molded the character of Lee Harvey Oswald there emerged a man capable of assassinating President Kennedy.

The proceedings of the commission were closed, though not secret, and about 3% of its files have yet to be released to the public, which has continued to provoke speculation among researchers.

Ramsey Clark Panel

In 1968, the Ramsey Clark Panel examined various photographs, X-ray films, documents, and other evidence, concluding that Kennedy was struck by two bullets fired from above and behind him, one of which traversed the base of the neck on the right side without striking bone, and the other of which entered the skull from behind and destroyed its right side.

House Select Committee

Main article: United States House Select Committee on Assassinations

Further information: Dictabelt evidence relating to the assassination of John F. Kennedy

In 1979, after a review of the evidence and of prior investigations, the United States House Select Committee on Assassinations was preparing to issue[*citation needed*] a finding that Oswald had acted alone in killing Kennedy. However, late in the Committee's proceedings a Dictabelt was introduced,Wikipedia:Please clarify purportedly recording sounds heard in Dealey Plaza before, during and after the shots were fired. After submitting the Dictabelt to acoustic analysis, the Committee revised its findings to assert a "high probability that two gunman fired" at Kennedy and that Kennedy "was probably assassinated as the result of a conspiracy." Although the Committee was "unable to identify the other gunman or the extent of the conspiracy," it made a number of further findings regarding the likelihood or unlikelihood that particular groups, named in the findings, were involved.

The Dictabelt evidence has been questioned, some believing it is not a recording of the assassination at all. The staff director and chief counsel for the Committee, G. Robert Blakey, told ABC NewsWikipedia:Manual_of_Style_(dates_and_numbers)#Chronological_items that at least 20 persons heard a shot from the grassy knoll, and that a conspiracy was established by both the witness testimony and acoustic evidence, but in 2004 he expressed less confidence. Officer H.B. McLain, from whose motorcycle radio the HSCA acoustic experts said the Dictabelt evidence came, has repeatedly stated that he was not yet in Dealey Plaza at the time of the assassination. McLain asked the Committee, "'If it was my radio on my motorcycle, why did it not record the revving up at high speed plus my siren when we immediately took off for Parkland Hospital?'"

In 1982, a group of twelve scientists appointed by the National Academy of Sciences (NAS), led by Norman Ramsey, concluded that the acoustic evidence submitted to the HSCA was "seriously flawed."[*citation needed*] Subsequently, a 2001 article in *Science and Justice*, the journal of Britain's Forensic Science Society, said that the NAS investigation was itself flawed and concluded with a 96.3 percent certainty that there were at least two gunmen firing at President Kennedy and that at least one shot came from the grassy knoll. Commenting on the British study, G. Robert Blakey said: "This is an honest, careful scientific examination of everything we did, with all the appropriate statistical checks."

Other investigations and dissenting theories

Main article: Kennedy assassination conspiracy theories

Critics have not accepted the conclusions of the Warren Commission and have proposed a number of other theories, such as that Oswald conspired with others, or was not involved at all and was framed.

In October 1981, with Marina's support, Oswald's grave was opened to test a theory propounded by writer Michael Eddowes: that during Oswald's stay in the Soviet Union he was replaced with a Soviet double; that it was this double, not Oswald, who killed Kennedy and who is buried in Oswald's grave; and that the exhumed remains would therefore not exhibit a surgical scar Oswald was known to carry. However, dental records positively identified the exhumed corpse as Oswald's, and the scar was present.

Image CE-133A, one of three known "backyard photos," the same image sent by Oswald (as a first-generation copy) to George de Mohrenschildt in April, 1963, dated and signed on the back. Oswald holds a Carcano rifle, with markings matching those on the rifle found in the Book Depository after the assassination.

Fictional trials

Several films have fictionalized a trial of Oswald. In 1986, a 21-hour unscripted mock trial was "held" on television, argued by actual lawyers before an actual judge, with unscripted testimony from surviving witnesses to the events surrounding the assassination; the mock jury returned a verdict of guilty. Author Gerald Posner (whose book *Case Closed* endorses the Warren Commission's conclusions) participatedWikipedia:Please clarify in a shorter, scripted mock trial for television.[citation needed]

Backyard photos

Main article: John F. Kennedy assassination rifle

Lee Harvey Oswald's Carcano rifle, in the US National Archives

The "backyard photos", taken by Marina Oswald probably around March 31, 1963 using a camera belonging to Oswald, show Oswald holding two Marxist newspapers—*The Militant* and *The Worker*—and a rifle, and wearing a pistol in a holster. Shown the pictures after his arrest, Oswald insisted they were forgeries, but Marina testified in 1964 that she had taken the photographs at Oswald's request— testimony she reaffirmed repeatedly over the decades. These photos were labelled CE 133-A and CE 133-B. CE 133-A shows the rifle in Oswald's left hand and newsletters in front of his chest in the other, while the rifle is held with the right hand in CE 133-B. Oswald's mother testified that on the day after the assassination she and Marina destroyed another photograph with Oswald holding the rifle with both hands over his head, with "To my daughter June" written on it.

The HSCA obtained another first generation print (from CE 133-A) on April 1, 1977 from the widow of George de Mohrenschildt. The words "Hunter of fascists — ha ha ha!" written in block Russian were on the back. Also in English were added in script: "To my friend George, Lee Oswald, 5/IV/63 [April 5, 1963]" Handwriting experts for the HSCA concluded the English inscription and signature were by Oswald. After two original photos, one negative and one first-generation copy had been found, the Senate Intelligence Committee located (in 1976) a third backyard photo (CE 133-C) showing Oswald with newspapers held away from his body in his right hand). A test photo by the Dallas Police of a stand-in in the identical pose was released with the Warren Commission evidence in 1964, but it is not known why CE 133-C itself was not publicly acknowledged until a print was found in 1975 amongst the effects of a deceased Dallas police officer.

These photos, widely recognized as some of the most significant evidence against Oswald, have been subjected to rigorous analysis. Photographic experts consulted by the HSCA concluded they were genuine, answering twenty-one points raised by critics. Marina Oswald has always maintained she took the photos herself, and the 1963 de Mohrenschildt print bearing Oswald's signature clearly indicate they existed before the assassination. Nonetheless, some continue to contest their authenticity. After digitally analyzing the photograph of Oswald holding the rifle and paper, computer scientist Hany Farid concluded that it "almost certainly was not altered."

Further reading

- Bugliosi, Vincent. *Reclaiming History: The Assassination of President John F. Kennedy*. Norton, 2007, 1632 p. ISBN 0393045250.
- Eddowes, Michael. *Khrushchev Killed Kennedy*, self-published, (1975), paperback (republished as *November 22, How They Killed Kennedy*, Neville Spearman (1976), hardback, ISBN 0-85978-019-8 and as *The Oswald File*, Potter (1977), hardcover, ISBN 0-517-53055-4)
- Groden, Robert J.. *The Search of Lee Harvey Oswald: A Comprehensive Photographic Record*, New York: Penguin Studio Books, 1995. ISBN 0-670-85867-6
- La Fontaine, Ray and Mary, "Oswald Talked: The New Evidence in the JFK Assassination", Gretna: Pelican Publishing Co., 1996. ISBN 1-56554-029-8
- Lambert, Patricia. *False Witness: The Real Story of Jim Garrison's Investigation and Oliver Stone's Film* JFK, New York: M. Evans & Company, 1998, ISBN 0-87131-920-9
- Lifton, David S., *Best Evidence: Disguise and Deception in the. Assassination of John F. Kennedy*, Carroll & Graf Publishers, NYC, 1988, softcover, ISBN 0-88184-438-1

- Mailer, Norman. *Oswald's Tale: An American Mystery*, New York: Ballantine Books, (1995) ISBN 0-345-40437-8
- Marrs, Jim. *Crossfire: The Plot That Killed Kennedy,* New York: Carroll & Graf Publishers, 1990, ISBN 0-88184-648-1
- McMillan, Priscilla Johnson. *Marina and Lee*, New York: Harper & Row, 1977.
- Melanson, Philip H. *Spy Saga: Lee Harvey Oswald And U. S. Intelligence*, Praeger Publishing, 1990, ISBN 0-275-93571-X
- Newman, John. *Oswald and the CIA*, New York: Carroll & Graf Publishers, 1995, ISBN 0-7867-0131-5
- Nechiporenko, Oleg M. *Passport to Assassination: The Never-Before Told Story of Lee Harvey Oswald by the KGB Colonel Who Knew Him*, New York: Carroll & Graf Publishers, 1993, ISBN 1-559-72210-X
- Posner, Gerald. *Case Closed: Lee Harvey Oswald and the Assassination of JFK*, Random House, 1993, hardcover, ISBN 0-679-41825-3
- Smith, Matthew. *JFK: Say Goodbye to America*, Mainstream Publishing, 2004.
- Smith, Matthew, *JFK: The Second Plot*. Mainstream Publishing.Edinburgh and London. 2000. ISBN 1-84018-501-5
- Summers, Anthony. *Conspiracy*, London: Fontana Books, 1980.
- Summers, Anthony. *Not in Your Lifetime*, New York: Marlowe & Company, 1998, ISBN 1-56924-739-0
- Douglass, James W. (2008). JFK and the Unspeakable: Why He Died and Why It Matters. Maryknoll, New York: Orbis Books. pp. 544. ISBN 9781570757556. http://www.maryknollmall.org/description.cfm?ISBN=978-1-57075-755-6.
- Wilkes, Jr., Donald E. "Lee Harvey Oswald at Age 62." [1] *Flagpole Magazine*, p. 6 (November 21, 2001).
- Wilkes, Jr., Donald E. "The Rosetta Stone of the JFK Assassination?" [2] *Flagpole Magazine*, p. 8 (November 20, 2002).

External links
- *Frontline*: Who Was Lee Harvey Oswald? [3]
- *American Experience*: Oswald's Ghost [4]
- Lee Harvey Oswald's journey from Minsk to the US, travelling through Holland [5] by Perry Vermeulen
- JFK 101 An excerpt from *Harvey & Lee: How the CIA Framed Oswald* [6] by John Armstrong
- Kennedy Assassination Home Page [7] by John McAdams
- Lasting Questions about the Murder of President Kennedy [8] by Rex Bradford
- Lee Harvey Oswald: Lone Assassin or Patsy [9]

- Lee Harvey Oswald Chronology [10]
- Crime Library: Lee Harvey Oswald [11]
- Lee Harvey Oswald In Russia [12]
- Various photos of Oswald taken post mortem [13]
- CTKA: Citizens for Truth about the Kennedy Assassination [14]
- Hasty Judgment: A Reply to Gerald Posner--Why the JFK Case Is Not Closed [15] by Michael T. Griffith
- Lee Harvey Oswald [16] at Find a Grave Retrieved on 2009-02-13

John F. Kennedy assassination conspiracy theories

There has long been suspicion of a government cover-up of information about the assassination of John F. Kennedy on November 22, 1963. There are also many **conspiracy theories regarding the assassination** that arose soon after his death and continue to be promoted today. Most put forth a criminal conspiracy involving parties as varied as the CIA, the KGB, the American Mafia, Israeli government, FBI director J. Edgar Hoover, sitting Vice President Lyndon B. Johnson, Cuban president Fidel Castro, anti-Castro Cuban exile groups, the Federal Reserve, or some combination of those entities and individuals.

President Kennedy, Jackie Kennedy, Nellie Connally and Governor John Connally, shortly before the assassination.

Background

President John F. Kennedy was assassinated as he traveled in an open top car in a motorcade in Dallas, Texas at 12:30 PM, November 22, 1963; Texas Governor John Connally was also injured. Within two hours, Lee Harvey Oswald was arrested for the murder of Dallas policeman J.D. Tippit and arraigned that evening. At 1:35 AM Saturday, Oswald was arraigned for murdering the President. At 11:21 AM, Sunday, November 24, 1963, nightclub owner Jack Ruby shot and killed Oswald as he was being transferred to the county jail.

In 1964, the Warren Commission concluded that there was no persuasive evidence that Oswald was involved in a conspiracy to assassinate the President, and stated their belief that he acted alone. Critics, even before the publication of the official government conclusions, suggested a conspiracy was behind the assassination. Though the public initially accepted the Warren Commission's conclusions, by 1966 the tide had turned as authors such as Mark Lane with his best-selling book *Rush to Judgment*, and prominent publications such as the New York Review of Books and Life openly disputed the findings of the commission.

Handbill circulated on November 21, 1963, one day before the assassination of John F. Kennedy.

In 1979, the House Select Committee on Assassinations (HSCA) agreed with the Warren Commission that Oswald assassinated Kennedy but found its report and the original FBI investigation to be seriously flawed. The HSCA also concluded that at least four shots were fired, that with "high probability" two gunmen fired at the President, and a conspiracy was probable. The HSCA also stated that "the Warren Commission failed to investigate adequately the possibility of a conspiracy to assassinate the President."

The Ramsey Clark Panel and the Rockefeller Commission both supported the Warren Commission's conclusions, while New Orleans District Attorney Jim Garrison unsuccessfully prosecuted Clay Shaw of conspiring to assassinate Kennedy.

Public opinion

Polls show many Americans believe there was a conspiracy to kill President Kennedy. These same polls also show that there is no agreement on who else may have been involved.

A 2003, Gallup poll reported that 75% of Americans do not believe that Lee Harvey Oswald acted alone. That same year an ABC News poll found that 70% of respondents suspected that the assassination involved more than one person. A 2004 Fox News poll found that 66% of Americans thought there had been a conspiracy while 74% thought there had been a cover-up.

Possible evidence of a cover-up

Numerous researchers, including Mark Lane, Henry Hurt, Michael L. Kurtz, Gerald D. McKnight and others have pointed out inconsistencies, oversights, exclusions of evidence, errors, changing stories, or changes made to witness testimony in the official Warren Commission investigation, which could suggest a cover-up, without putting forward a theory as to who actually committed the murder.

Alleged murder weapon

One example of a changing story involves the alleged murder weapon. Deputy Sheriff Eugene Boone and Deputy Constable Seymour Weitzman both initially identified the rifle found in the Dallas School Book Depository as a 7.65 Mauser. Weitzman signed an affidavit the following day describing the weapon as a "7.65 Mauser bolt action equipped with a 4/18 scope, a thick leather brownish-black sling on it". Deputy Sheriff Roger Craig claimed that he saw "7.65 Mauser" stamped on the barrel of the weapon.

Dallas District Attorney Henry Wade told the press that the weapon found in the School Book Depository was a 7.65 Mauser, and this was reported by the news media. But investigators later identified the rifle as a 6.5 Italian Mannlicher Carcano. According to Mark Lane:

> "The strongest element in the case against Lee Harvey Oswald was the Warren Commission's conclusion that his rifle had been found on the 6th floor of the Book Depository building. Yet Oswald never owned a 7.65 Mauser. When the FBI later reported that Oswald had purchased only a 6.5 Italian Mannlicher-Carcano, the weapon at police headquarters in Dallas miraculously changed its (caliber), its make and its nationality. The Warren Commission concluded that a 6.5 Mannlicher-Carcano, not a 7.65 German Mauser, had been discovered by the Dallas deputies."

Witness intimidation allegations

Some witnesses to the assassination, or to events connected to the assassination, were intimidated or threatened. These include Jean Hill, Richard Carr, Roy Truly, Sandy Speaker, and A. J. Millican. Acquilla Clemmons, who claimed she saw two men at the scene of Officer J.D. Tippit's murder, also claimed she was told to keep quiet about what she saw by a man with a gun who came to her home.

Suspicious or unexplained witness deaths

Jim Marrs and Ralph Schuster have pointed out what they have characterized as a suspiciously large number of deaths of people connected with the investigation of the assassination. They also point out that there seems to be a pattern of deaths around the times of various government investigations, such as during and just after the Warren Commission investigation, as New Orleans District Attorney Jim Garrison was launching his own investigation, while the Senate Intelligence Committee was looking into assassinations by U.S. intelligence agencies in the 1970s, and when the House Select Committee on Assassinations was gearing up its investigations. Marrs points out that "these deaths certainly would have been convenient for anyone not wishing the truth of the JFK assassination to become public."

Withheld documents

Many government records relating to the assassination, including some from the Warren Commission investigation, the House Special Committee on Assassinations investigation and the Church Committee investigation, were kept secret from the public. These secret documents included the president's autopsy records. Some were not scheduled to be released until 2029, however many of these documents were released during the mid to late 1990s by the Assassination Records Review Board due to the *President John F. Kennedy Assassination Records Collection Act of 1992*. Some of the material released contains redacted sections. Tax return information, which would identify employers and sources of income, has not been released. The existence of large numbers of secret documents related to the assassination, and the long period of secrecy, suggests to some the possibility of a cover-up. One historian noted, "There exists widespread suspicion about the government's disposition of the Kennedy assassination records stemming from the beliefs that Federal officials (1) have not made available all Government assassination records (even to the Warren Commission, Church Committee, House Assassination Committee) and (2) have heavily redacted the records released under FOIA in order to cover up sinister conspiracies." According to the Assassination Records Review Board, "All Warren Commission records, except those records that contain tax return information, are (now) available to the public with only minor redactions."

Autopsy

There is conflicting testimony about the autopsy performed on President Kennedy's body, particularly as to when the examination of the president's brain took place, who was present, and whether or not the photos submitted as evidence are the same as those taken during the examination. Douglas Horne, the Assassination Record Review Board's chief analyst for military records, said he was "90 to 95% certain" that the photographs in the National Archives are not of President Kennedy's brain. Dr. Gary Aguilar, assisted by pathologist Dr. Cyril Wecht, wrote in a 1999 piece for *The Consortium News*, "According to Horne's findings, the second brain -- which showed an exit wound in the front -- allegedly replaced Kennedy's real brain -- which revealed much greater damage to the rear, consistent with an exit wound and thus evidence of a shot from the front."

James H. Fetzer has noted 16 problems with the Warren Commission's version of events, which he claims prove decisively that its narrative is impossible, and therefore is likely a cover-up. He claims that evidence released by the Assassination Records Review Board substantiates these concerns. These include problems with bullet trajectories, the alleged murder weapon, the alleged ammunition used, inconsistencies between the Warren Commission's account and the autopsy findings, inconsistencies between the autopsy findings and what was observed by witnesses at the scene of the murder, eye-witness accounts that conflict with x-rays supposedly taken of the President's body, indications that the diagrams and photos of the President's brain in the National Archives are not the President's, testimony by those who took and processed the autopsy photos that the photos were altered, created or destroyed, indications that the Zapruder film has been tampered with, allegations that the Warren Commission's version of events conflicts with news reports from the scene of the murder, the change in the motorcade route that by an incredible coincidence brought the President right to the place where the ambush was set, inexplicably lax Secret Service and local law enforcement security, and confessions by people who claim that they had knowledge of, or participated in, a conspiracy to kill the President.

Physician Malcolm Perry described the original throat wound as "a very small injury, with clear cut, although somewhat irregular margins of less than a quarter inch in diameter, with minimal tissue damage surrounding it on the skin".

Conspiracy theories

More than one gunman

The Warren Commission findings and the single bullet theory are implausible according to some researchers. Oswald's rifle, through testing performed by the FBI, could only be fired three times within five to eight seconds. The Warren Commission, through eyewitnesses, determined that only three bullets were fired as well: one of the three bullets missed the vehicle entirely; one hit Kennedy and passed through Governor John Connally, and the third bullet was fatal to the President. The weight of the bullet fragments taken from Connally and those remaining in his body supposedly totaled more than could have been missing from the bullet found on Connally's stretcher, known as the "magic bullet". However, witness testimony seems to indicate that only tiny fragments, of less total mass than was missing from the bullet, were left in Connally. In addition, the trajectory of the bullet, which hit Kennedy above the right shoulder blade and passed through his neck (according to the autopsy), supposedly would have had to change course to pass through Connally's rib cage and wrist. In the Zapruder film Kennedy appears to move backwards in the last, fatal shot. Claims have been made that suggest his head jerks forward and then backwards.

Dealey Plaza in 2003.

The wooden fence on the grassy knoll.

Other evidence for the claim of more than three shots fired was the FBI photographs of the limousines, showing a bullet hole in the windshield of the vehicle above the rear-view mirror. The Warren Commission ignored the evidence. The Government's response was that it "occurred prior to Dallas".

Witnesses

Thirty-five witnesses, some 32% of those who were eye-witnesses to the shooting, thought that shots were fired from somewhere in front of the President — from the area of the Grassy Knoll or Triple Underpass — while 56 eyewitnesses thought the shots came from the Depository, or at least in that direction, behind the President, and 5 witnesses thought that the shots came from two directions.

Nellie Connally was sitting in the presidential car next to her husband, Governor John Connally. In her book *From Love Field: Our Final Hours*, Connally was adamant that her husband was hit by a bullet that was separate from the two that hit Kennedy.

Roy Kellerman, a U.S. Secret Service Agent, testified that, "Now, in the seconds that I talked just now, a flurry of shells come into the car." Kellerman said that he saw a 5-inch-diameter (130 mm) hole in the back right-hand side of the President's head.

Lee Bowers was operating a railroad interlocking tower, overlooking the parking lot just north of the grassy knoll and west of the Texas School Book Depository. He reported that he saw two men behind the picket fence at the top of the grassy knoll before the shooting. When interviewed by Mark Lane, Bowers noted that he saw something that attracted his attention, either a flash of light, or maybe smoke, from the knoll, leading him to believe "something out of the ordinary" had occurred there. Bowers was cut off while giving testimony to the Warren Commission. Bowers told Lane he heard three shots, the last two in quick succession. Bowers was of the opinion that they could not have come from the same rifle.

Clint Hill, the Secret Service Agent who was sheltering the President with his body on the way to the hospital, described "The right rear portion of his head was missing. It was lying in the rear seat of the car." Later, to a National Geographic documentary film crew, he described the large defect in the skull as "gaping hole above his right ear, about the size of my palm."

Robert McClelland, a physician in the emergency room who observed the head wound, testified that the back right part of the head was blown out with posterior cerebral tissue and some of the cerebellar tissue was missing. The size of the back head wound, according to his description, indicated it was an exit wound, and that a second shooter from the front delivered the fatal head shot, or the president had his head turned.

Rose Cherami (sometimes spelled "Cheramie") was depicted in Oliver Stone's 1991 movie *JFK* as a "witness." Rose Cherami was a 41-year-old drug addict and prostitute who was picked up on Highway 190 near Eunice, Louisiana, on November 20, 1963—two days before the Kennedy assassination—by Lt. Francis Frugé of the Louisiana State Police. Cherami told Frugé that John F. Kennedy would shortly be killed. Fruge did not believe her at first, but after some time of adamant speaking by Cherami, he came around. During her confinement, and prior to the time JFK was shot in Dallas, Cherami supposedly spoke of the impending assassination. After Jack Ruby shot Lee Harvey Oswald, Cherami reportedly claimed that she had worked for Ruby as a stripper, that she knew both Ruby and Oswald, and that the two men were "bed partners" who "had been shacking up for years." According to Lt. Frugé, Cherami declined to repeat her story to the FBI. She was killed when struck by a car on September 4, 1965, apparently while hitchhiking, near Gladewater, Texas. Among conspiracy theorists, the story has been considered quite credible since 1979, when an account by investigator Patricia Orr was published by the House Select Committee reviewing the JFK assassination (HSCA). This account was based primarily on the HSCA depositions of Francis Frugé and Victor Weiss, a doctor at the Jackson hospital.

Suspects in Dealey Plaza other than Oswald

Numerous witnesses reported hearing gunfire coming from the Dal-Tex Building, which is located across the street from the Texas School Book Depository and in alignment with Elm Street in Dealey Plaza. Several conspiracy theories posit that at least one shooter was located in the Dal-Tex Building due to witness accounts and other coincidences including the apprehension of suspicious individuals like the "man in black leather" and ex-con Jim Braden inside the building, as well as the trajectory of the bullet which hit the curb on the south end of Dealey Plaza injuring bystander James Tague. Also of note is the scientific acoustic evidence presented to the House Select Committee on Assassinations in 1978 which pinpointed the Dal-Tex building as a possible source of gunfire.

Analysis

Former U.S. Marine sniper Craig Roberts and Gunnery Sergeant Carlos Hathcock, who was the senior instructor for the U.S. Marine Corps Sniper Instructor School at Marine Corps Base Quantico in Quantico, Virginia, both said it could not be done as described by the FBI investigators. "Let me tell you what we did at Quantico," Hathcock said. "We reconstructed the whole thing: the angle, the range, the moving target, the time limit, the obstacles, everything. I don't know how many times we tried it, but we couldn't duplicate what the Warren Commission said Oswald did. Now if I can't do it, how in the world could a guy who was a non-qual on the rifle range and later only qualified 'marksman' do it?"

Kennedy's death certificate located the bullet at the third thoracic vertebra — which some claim is too low to have exited his throat. Moreover, the bullet was traveling downward, since the shooter was by a sixth floor window. The autopsy cover sheet had a diagram of a body showing this same low placement at the third thoracic vertebra. The hole in back of Kennedy's shirt and jacket are also claimed to support a wound too low to be consistent with the Single Bullet Theory.

New Orleans conspiracy

Further information: Trial of Clay Shaw, People involved in the trial of Clay Shaw, and David Ferrie

Immediately following the assassination, allegations began to surface of a conspiracy between Oswald and persons with whom he was or may have been acquainted while he lived in New Orleans, Louisiana.

On November 25, 1963 (the day after Oswald's murder by Jack Ruby) Dean Andrews, Jr., a New Orleans attorney who had occasionally provided legal advice to Oswald, informed the FBI that two days earlier he had, while in a local hospital under sedation, received a telephone call from a man named Clay Bertrand who inquired if he would be willing to defend Oswald in the murder and assassination case. Andrews later repeated these claims in testimony to the Warren Commission.

Also in late November 1963 an employee of New Orleans private investigator Guy Banister named Jack Martin began making accusations of possible involvement in the assassination by fellow Banister employee David Ferrie. According to witnesses, in 1963 Ferrie and Banister were working for lawyer

G. Wray Gill, on behalf of Gill's client, New Orleans Mafia boss Carlos Marcello. Ferrie had also attended Civil Air Patrol meetings in New Orleans in the 1950s that were also attended by a teenage Lee Harvey Oswald.

In 1966, New Orleans D.A. Jim Garrison began an investigation into the assassination of President Kennedy. Garrison's investigation led him to conclude that Kennedy had been assassinated as the result of a conspiracy involving Oswald, David Ferrie and "Clay Bertrand." Garrison further came to believe "Clay Bertrand" was a pseudonym for New Orleans businessman Clay Shaw. On March 1, 1967, Garrison arrested and charged Shaw with conspiring to assassinate President Kennedy, with the help of Lee Harvey Oswald, David Ferrie, and others. On January 29, 1969, Clay Shaw was brought to trial on these charges, and the jury found him not guilty.

In 2003, Judyth Vary Baker, a former employee of the Reily Coffee Company in New Orleans who had been employed there at the same time as Lee Harvey Oswald, appeared in an episode of Nigel Turner's ongoing documentary television series, *The Men Who Killed Kennedy*. According to Baker, she and Oswald had been hired by Reily in the spring of 1963 as a "cover" for a clandestine CIA project designed to develop biological weapons that could be used to assassinate Fidel Castro. Baker further claimed that she and Oswald began an affair, and that they had planned to run away to Mexico together after the assassination. In the years since Baker first made her allegations public, she has failed to produce any evidence that she was acquainted with Oswald, and the research community has widely concluded that her claims are a hoax.

Federal Reserve conspiracy

Jim Marrs, in his book *Crossfire: The Plot That Killed Kennedy*, speculated that the assassination of Kennedy might have been motivated by the issuance of Executive Order 11110. This executive order enabled the Treasury to print silver certificates, bypassing the Federal Reserve System. Executive Order 11110 was not officially repealed until the Ronald Reagan Administration. Official explanations claim that the executive order was simply an attempt to drain the silver reserves, and did not actually endanger the careers of anyone working at the Federal Reserve.

This theory was further explored by U.S. Marine sniper and veteran police officer Craig Roberts in the 1994 book, *Kill Zone*. Roberts theorized that the Executive Order was the beginning of a plan by Kennedy whose ultimate goal was to permanently do away with the United States Federal Reserve, and that Kennedy was murdered by a cabal of international bankers determined to foil this plan.

Actor and author Richard Belzer has also discussed this theory. According to Belzer the plot to kill Kennedy was set in motion as a response to the President's attempt to shift power away from the Federal Reserve and to the U.S Treasury Department.

Three tramps

Nearly a dozen people were taken into custody in and around Dealey Plaza in the minutes following the assassination. In most of these instances, no records of the identities of those detained were kept. The most famous of those taken into custody have come to be known as the "tramps": three men discovered in a boxcar in the rail yard west of the grassy knoll. Speculation regarding the identities of the three and their possible involvement in the assassination became widespread in the ensuing years. Photographs of the three at their time of arrest fueled this speculation, as the three "tramps" appeared to be well-dressed and clean-shaven, seemingly unlikely for hobos riding the rails. Some researchers also thought it suspicious that the Dallas police had quickly released the tramps from custody apparently without investigating whether they might have witnessed anything significant related to the assassination, and that Dallas police claimed to have lost the records of their arrests as well as their mugshots and fingerprints.

In 1989, the Dallas police department released a large collection of files that contained the arrest records of the three men, whose names were Harold Doyle of Red Jacket, West Virginia; John F. Gedney, with no listed home address; and Gus W. Abrams, also with no listed home address. The brief report described the men as "all passing through [Dallas]. They have no jobs, etc." and were known to be rail-riders in the area. The previous evening they had slept in a homeless shelter where they showered and shaved, explaining their clean appearance on the day of the assassination. The three were released from custody four days after the assassination on the morning of November 26.

When asked in a 1992 interview, Doyle said that he had deliberately avoided revealing himself to the public limelight, saying, "I am a plain guy, a simple country boy, and that's the way I want to stay. I wouldn't be a celebrity for $10 million." Gedney independently affirmed Doyle's sentiment. Abrams had since died (in Ohio in 1987), but his sister also corroborated the events of that day and noted that Abrams "was always on the go, hopping trains and drinking wine." The three were evidently not involved in the assassination in any way.

A list of the better known "identifications" of the three tramps alleged by conspiracy theorists includes:

Charles Harrelson, the father of actor Woody Harrelson, has been alleged to be the tallest of the three tramps in the photographs. Harrelson at various times before his death boasted about his role as one of the tramps, however, in a 1988 interview, he denied being in Dallas on the day of the assassination.

E. Howard Hunt, the CIA station chief who was instrumental in the Bay of Pigs Invasion, and who later worked as one of President Richard Nixon's White House Plumbers, was alleged by some to be the oldest of the tramps. At the time of his death, Hunt's son released tapes of Hunt implicating LBJ in Kennedy's assassination. In 1975, Hunt testified to the United States President's Commission on CIA activities within the United States that he was in Washington, D.C. on the day of the assassination. This testimony was confirmed by Hunt's family and a home employee of the Hunts. In 1985 however, in Hunt's libel suit against *Liberty Lobby*, defense attorney Mark Lane introduced doubt as to Hunt's location on the day of the Kennedy assassination through depositions from David Atlee Phillips,

Richard Helms, G. Gordon Liddy, Stansfield Turner, and Marita Lorenz, plus a cross-examination of Hunt.

Frank Sturgis is thought by some to be the tall tramp in the photographs. Like Hunt, Sturgis was involved both in the Bay of Pigs invasion and the Watergate burglary. In 1959, Sturgis became involved with Marita Lorenz, who later identified Sturgis as a gunman in the assassination. Hunt's confessions before his death similarly implicates Sturgis.

Chauncey Holt, also alleged by some to be the oldest of the tramps, claims to have been a double agent for the CIA and the Mafia, and has claimed that his assignment in Dallas was to provide fake Secret Service credentials to people in the vicinity. Witness reports state that there were one or more unidentified men in the area claiming to be Secret Service agents.

The House Select Committee on Assassinations had forensic anthropologists study the photographic evidence. They were able to rule out E. Howard Hunt, Frank Sturgis, Dan Carswell, Fred Lee Chapman, and other suspects in 1978. The Rockefeller Commission concluded that neither Hunt nor Frank Sturgis was in Dallas on the day of the assassination.

Despite these positive identifications of the tramps and the lack of any connection between them and the assassination, some have maintained their identifications of the three as persons other than Doyle, Gedney and Abrams and have continued to theorize that they may have been connected to the crime.

CIA conspiracy

Some researchers have claimed that CIA officer David Atlee Phillips used the alias "Maurice Bishop." He used the pseudonym while working with Alpha 66, an organization of anti-Castro Cubans. Alpha 66's founder, Antonio Veciana, claimed that during one of his meetings with "Bishop", Lee Harvey Oswald was also in attendance. HSCA investigator Gaeton Fonzi believed Phillips was Bishop.

In 1995, former U.S. Army Intelligence officer and National Security Agency executive assistance John M. Newman published evidence that both the CIA and FBI had deliberately tampered with their files on Lee Harvey Oswald both before and after the assassination. Furthermore, he found that both had withheld information that might have alerted authorities in Dallas that Oswald posed a potential threat to the President. Subsequently, Newman has expressed a belief that James Angleton was probably the key figure in the assassination. According to Newman, only Angleton, "had the access, the authority, and the diabolically ingenious mind to manage this sophisticated plot."

See also: CIA Kennedy assassination conspiracy theory

Secret Service conspiracy

The House Select Committee on Assassinations concluded that although Oswald assassinated Kennedy, a conspiracy was probable. Among its findings, the HSCA noted that President Kennedy had not received adequate protection in Dallas, that the Secret Service possessed information that was not properly analyzed, investigated or used by the Secret Service in connection with the President's trip to Dallas, and finally that the Secret Service agents in the motorcade were inadequately prepared to protect the President from a sniper. Although widely disputed but possible, this lack of protection may have occurred because Kennedy himself had specifically asked that the Secret Service make itself discreet during the Dallas visit.

Cuban exiles

Richard Helms, a director of the CIA's Office of Special Operations, had reason to be hostile to Kennedy since when first elected, Kennedy supported invading Cuba and then only later changed his mind about how to approach the matter. After the disastrous Bay of Pigs Invasion of Cuba sponsored by the CIA, Kennedy changed his mind about an invasion, earning the hatred of the Cuban exile community. Thus, Helms was immediately put under pressure from President Kennedy and his brother Robert (the Attorney General) to increase American efforts to get rid of the Castro regime. Operation Mongoose had nearly 4,000 operators involved in attacks on Cuban economic targets.

The House Select Committee on Assassinations believed evidence existed implicating certain violent Cuban exiles may have participated in Kennedy's murder. These exiles worked closely with CIA operatives in violent activities against Castro's Cuba. In 1979, the committee reported this:

> President Kennedy's popularity among the Cuban exiles had plunged deeply by 1963. Their bitterness is illustrated in a tape recording of a meeting of anti-Castro Cubans and right-wing Americans in the Dallas suburb of Farmer's Branch on October 1, 1963. (37)

Holding a copy of the September 26 edition of *The Dallas Morning News*, featuring a front-page account of the President's planned trip to Texas in November, the Cuban exile vented his hostility:

> "CASTELLANOS... we're waiting for Kennedy the 22d, [the date Kennedy was murdered] buddy. We're going to see him in one way or the other. We're going to give him the works when he gets in Dallas. Mr. good ol' Kennedy. I wouldn't even call him President Kennedy. He stinks."

Author Joan Didion explored the Miami anti-Castro Cuban theory in her 1987 non-fiction book "Miami." In "Miami," she emphasizes the questions that investigators raised to Marita Lorenz regarding Guillermo Novo, a Cuban exile who was involved in shooting a bazooka at the U.N. building from the East River during a speech by Che Guevara. Allegedly, Novo was affiliated with Lee Harvey Oswald and Frank Sturgis and carried weapons with them to a hotel in Dallas just prior to the assassination. These claims, though put forth to the House Assassinations Committee by Lorenz, were never substantiated by a conclusive investigation.

E. Howard Hunt

Former CIA agent and Watergate figure E. Howard Hunt has been named as a possible participant in several Kennedy assassination conspiracy theories. Separately, he denied complicity in the murder of JFK while accusing others of being involved.

Some researchers have identified Hunt as a figure crossing Dealey Plaza in a raincoat and fedora immediately after the assassination. Others have suggested that Hunt was one of the men known as the three tramps who were arrested and then quickly released shortly after the assassination.

In 1976, a magazine called *The Spotlight* ran an article accusing Hunt of being in Dallas on November 22, 1963, and of having a role in the assassination. Hunt won a libel judgment against the magazine in 1981, but this was thrown out on appeal, and the magazine was found not guilty when the case was retried in 1985.

Shortly before his death in 2007, Hunt authored an autobiography which implicated Lyndon B. Johnson in the assassination. Hunt suggested that Johnson had orchestrated the killing with the help of CIA agents who had been angered by Kennedy's actions as President. A 2007 article published in *Rolling Stone* magazine revealed deathbed confessions by Hunt to his son which suggested a conspiracy to kill JFK orchestrated by Lyndon Johnson, CIA agents Cord Meyer, Bill Harvey and David Sánchez Morales, as well as a "French gunman" who purportedly shot at Kennedy from the grassy knoll.

Organized crime conspiracy

Mafia criminals may have wished to retaliate for increasing pressure put upon them by Robert Kennedy (who had increased by 12 times the number of prosecutions under President Dwight Eisenhower). Documents never seen by the Warren Commission have revealed that some Mafiosi were working very closely with the CIA on several assassination attempts of Fidel Castro.

Teamsters Union president Jimmy Hoffa, and mobsters Carlos Marcello, Sam Giancana, Johnny Roselli, Charles Nicoletti and Santo Trafficante Jr. (all of whom say Hoffa worked with the CIA on the Castro assassination plots) top the list of House Select Committee on Assassinations Mafia suspects. Giancana, Marcello, and Trafficante were the leading figures of the organized crime families in Chicago, New Orleans, and Tampa, respectively.

Carlos Marcello apparently threatened to assassinate the President to short-circuit his younger brother Bobby, who was serving as attorney general and leading the administration's anti-Mafia crusade.

In his memoir, *Bound by Honor: A Mafioso's Story*, Bill Bonanno, son of New York Mafia boss Joseph Bonanno explains that several Mafia families had long-standing ties with the anti-Castro Cubans through the Havana casinos operated by the Mafia before the Cuban Revolution. The Cubans hated Kennedy because he failed to fully support them in the Bay of Pigs Invasion; the Mafia hated the

Kennedys because, as Attorney General, the young and idealistic Robert Kennedy conducted an unprecedented legal assault on organized crime. This was especially provocative because several of the Mafia "families" had worked with JFK's father, Joseph Kennedy, to get JFK elected, and there was speculation about voting irregularities during the 1960 election. Both the Mafia and the anti-Castro Cubans were expert in assassination, the Cubans having been trained by the CIA. Bonanno reports that he realized the degree of the involvement of other Mafia families when he witnessed Jack Ruby killing Oswald on television: the Bonannos recognized Jack Ruby as an associate of Chicago mobster Sam Giancana.

Information released only around 2006 by the FBI indicates that Carlos Marcello confessed in detail to having organized Kennedy's assassination. The FBI then covered up this information which it had in its possession. This version of events is also supported by the findings of a 1979 Congressional Committee investigation that Marcello was likely part of a Mafia conspiracy behind the assassination, and had the means and the opportunity required. The assassination came less than a fortnight prior to a coup against Castro in Cuba by the Kennedy brothers, related to the Missile Crisis and Bay of Pigs Invasion.

James Files claims to be a former assassin working for both the Mafia and the CIA who participated in the assassination along with Johnny Roselli and Charles Nicoletti at the behest of Sam Giancana. He is currently serving a 30-year jail sentence for the attempted murder of a policeman.

Judith Campbell Exner, an alleged girlfriend of President Kennedy was also Sam Giancana's mistress; she was interviewed (apparently live) by Maria Shriver (daughter of Eunice Kennedy and Sargent Shriver) on ABC's *Good Morning America*. The woman was asked if she ever carried messages between JFK and Giancana because she knew them both. The woman confirmed that and said no to the question by saying, "Sam would never write anything down."[citation needed]

David Kaiser has also suggested mob involvement in his book, *The Road to Dallas*.

Famed investigative reporter Jack Anderson, who knew Kennedy well and had many sources within Organized Crime, concluded that Cuba and Fidel Castro worked with Organized Crime figures to arrange the assassination. In his book "Peace War and Politics," Anderson said Johnny Roselli gave him extensive details on the plot. Anderson said he was never able to independently confirm Roselli's entire story, but he wrote that many of Roselli's details checked out and he never found one detail that he could refute. Anderson said that whatever role Oswald played in the assassination, he was convinced that there was more than one gunman.

Lyndon Johnson conspiracy

In 2003, researcher Barr McClellan published the book, *Blood, Money & Power: How L.B.J. Killed J.F.K.*. McClellan claims that Lyndon Johnson, motivated by the fear of being dropped from the Kennedy ticket in 1964 and the need to cover up various scandals, masterminded Kennedy's assassination with the help of his friend attorney Edwardo Clark. The book suggests that a smudged partial fingerprint from the sniper's nest likely belonged to Johnson's associate Malcolm "Mac"

Wallace, and that Mac Wallace was therefore the assassin. The book further claims that the killing of Kennedy was paid for by oil magnates including Clint Murchison and H. L. Hunt. McClellan's book subsequently became the subject of an episode of Nigel Turner's ongoing documentary television series, *The Men Who Killed Kennedy*. The episode, entitled "The Guilty Men", drew widespread condemnation from both the Johnson family and President Johnson's former aides following its airing on The History Channel, which subsequently agreed not to air the episode in the future.

Madeleine D. Brown, who was an alleged mistress of Johnson, has also implicated him in a conspiracy to kill Kennedy. Brown alleged in 1997 that Johnson along with H. L. Hunt had begun planning Kennedy's demise as early as 1960. Brown claimed that by its fruition in 1963 the conspiracy involved dozens of persons including the leadership of FBI and the Mafia as well as well-known politicians and journalists. In the documentary *The Men Who Killed Kennedy*, Brown and a former employee of Clint Murchison both placed J. Edgar Hoover and LBJ at a dinner at Murchison's mansion shortly before the assassination. Brown claimed in the documentary that Johnson told her after the party that the Kennedys "will never embarrass me again."

Johnson was also accused of complicity in the assassination by former CIA agent and Watergate figure E. Howard Hunt.

American Fact-Finding Committee

Many researchers and conspiracy theorists talk about the full page, black-bordered advertisement published in the Nov 22, 1963 Dallas Morning News that accused Kennedy of ignoring the United States Constitution and implying that he was a communist. The ad was signed by the "American Fact-Finding Committee", Bernard Weissman, chairman. The FBI later investigated the source of funds for the ad, and interviewed many people involved, as described in the Warren Commission Hearings Volume XXIII. These people are many of the same discussed in the Lyndon Johnson theories and the allegations of Madeleine Brown (see above). Weissman was a supporter of the John Birch Society.

Soviet Bloc conspiracy

According to a 1966 FBI document, a source considered reliable by the Bureau related to the FBI in late 1963 that Colonel Boris Ivanov, Chief of the Soviet Committee for State Security (KGB), who resided in New York City at the time of the assassination, stated that it was his personal feeling that the assassination of President Kennedy had been planned by an organized group rather than being the act of one individual assassin.

Much later, the highest-ranking Soviet Bloc intelligence defector, Lt. Gen. Ion Mihai Pacepa described his conversation with Nicolae Ceaușescu who told him about "ten international leaders the Kremlin killed or tried to kill": "László Rajk and Imre Nagy of Hungary; Lucrețiu Pătrășcanu and Gheorghiu-Dej in Romania; Rudolf Slánský, the head of Czechoslovakia, and Jan Masaryk, that country's chief diplomat; the shah of Iran; Palmiro Togliatti of Italy; American President John F.

on to another procedure.' We jumped back and forth, back and forth. There was no smooth flow of procedure at all."

As done with all cargo on airplanes for safety, the coffin and lid were held by steel wrapping cables to prevent shifting during takeoff and landing and in case of air disturbances in flight. The casket was also under ample armed guard at all times, a fact that Lifton neglects to mention. In addition, the plane was watched by thousands of people that bathed the far side of the plane in lights and provided a very public stage for any body snatchers.

Other published theories

- James W. Douglass' *JFK and the Unspeakable* (2008) presents evidence that JFK was assassinated by elements within the US Government opposed to his attempts to end the Cold War through back channel negotiations with Khrushchev and Castro. ISBN 1-57075-755-0.

- *The Gemstone File: A Memoir* (2006), by Stephanie Caruana, posits that Oswald was part of a 28-man assassination team which included three U.S. Mafia hitmen (Jimmy Fratianno, John Roselli, and Eugene Brading). Oswald's role was to shoot John Connally. Bruce Roberts, author of the Gemstone File papers, claimed that the JFK assassination scenario was modeled after a supposed attempted assassination of President F.D. Roosevelt. Roosevelt was riding in an open car with Mayor Anton Cermak of Chicago. Cermak was shot and killed by Giuseppe Zangara. In Dallas, JFK was the real target, and Connally was a secondary target. The JFK assassination is only a small part of the Gemstone File's account. ISBN 1-4120-6137-7.

- David Wrone's *The Zapruder Film* (2003) concludes that the shot that killed JFK came from in front of the limousine, and that JFK's throat and back wounds were caused by an in-and-through shot originating from the grassy knoll. Three shots were fired from three different angles, none of them from Lee Harvey Oswald's window at the Texas School Book Depository. Wrone is a professor of history (emeritus) at the University of Wisconsin–Stevens Point. ISBN 0-7006-1291-2.

- *JFK: The Second Plot* (2002) by Matthew Smith explores the strange case of Roscoe White. In 1990, Roscoe's son Ricky made public a claim that his father, who had been a Dallas police officer in 1963, was involved in killing the president. Roscoe's widow Geneva also claimed that before her husband's death in 1971 he left a diary in which he revealed that he was one of the marksmen who shot the President, and that he also killed Officer J. D. Tippit. ISBN 1-84018-501-5.

- *The Kennedy Mutiny* (2002) by Will Fritz (not the same as police captain J. Will Fritz), claims that the assassination plot was orchestrated by General Edwin Walker, and that he framed Oswald for the crime. ISBN 0-9721635-0-6.

- Norman Mailer's *Oswald's Tale: An American Mystery* (1995) concludes that Oswald was guilty, but holds that the evidence may point to a second gunman on the grassy knoll, who, purely by coincidence, was attempting to kill JFK at the same time as Oswald. "If there was indeed another shot, it was not necessarily fired by a conspirator of Oswald's. Such a gun could have belonged to another lone killer or to a conspirator working for some other group altogether." ISBN 0-679-42535-7.

- *Passport to Assassination* (1993) by Oleg M. Nechiporenko, the Soviet consular official (and highly placed KGB officer) who met with Oswald in Mexico City in 1963. He was afforded the unique opportunity to interview Oswald about his goals including his genuine desire for a Cuban visa. His conclusions were (1) that Oswald killed Kennedy due to extreme feelings of inadequacy versus his wife's professed admiration for JFK, and (2) that the KGB never sought intelligence information from Oswald during his time in the USSR as they did not trust his motivations. ISBN 1-55972-210-X.

- *Who Shot JFK? : A Guide to the Major Conspiracy Theories* (1993) by Bob Callahan and Mark Zingarelli explores some of the more obscure theories regarding JFK's murder, such as "The Coca-Cola Theory." According this theory, suggested by the editor of an organic gardening magazine, Oswald killed JFK due to mental impairment stemming from an addiction to refined sugar, as evidenced by his need for his favorite beverage immediately after the assassination. ISBN 0-671-79494-9.

- *Mortal Error: The Shot That Killed JFK* (1992) by Bonar Menninger (ISBN 0-312-08074-3) alleges that while Oswald did attempt to assassinate JFK and did succeed in wounding him, the fatal shot was accidentally fired by Secret Service agent George Hickey, who was riding in the Secret Service follow-up car directly behind the Presidential Limousine. The theory alleges that after the first two shots were fired the motorcade sped up while Hickey was attempting to respond to Oswald's shots and he lost his balance and accidentally pulled the trigger of his AR-15 and shot JFK. Hickey's testimony says otherwise: "*At the end of the last report* (shot) I reached to the bottom of the car and picked up the AR 15 rifle, cocked and loaded it, *and turned to the rear.*" (italics added). George Hickey sued Menninger in April 1995 for what he had written in *Mortal Error*. The case was dismissed as its statute of limitations had run out.

- Mark North's *Act of Treason: The Role of J. Edgar Hoover in the assassination of President Kennedy,* (1991) implicates the FBI Director. North documents that Hoover was aware of threats against Kennedy by organized crime before 1963, and suggests that he failed to take proper action to prevent the assassination. North also charges Hoover with failure to work adequately to uncover the truth behind Kennedy's murder. ISBN 0-88184-877-8.

- *Reasonable Doubt* (1985) by Henry Hurt, who writes about his Warren Commission doubts. Mr. Hurt pins the plot on professional crook Robert Easterling, along with Texas oilmen and the supposed Ferrie/Shaw alliance. ISBN 0-03-004059-0.

- *Appointment in Dallas* (1975) by Hugh McDonald suggests that Oswald was lured into a plot that he was told was a staged fake attempt to kill JFK to embarrass the Secret Service and to alert the government of the necessity for beefed-up Secret Service security. Oswald's role was to shoot at the motorcade but deliberately miss the target. The plotters then killed JFK themselves and framed Oswald for the crime. McDonald claims that, after being told the "truth" about JFK's death by CIA agent Herman Kimsey in 1964, he spent years trying to locate a man known as "Saul." Saul was supposedly the unidentified man who was photographed exiting the Russian embassy in Mexico City in September 1963, whose photos were subsequently sent to the FBI in Dallas on the morning of November 22, 1963 (before the assassination), and mislabelled "Lee Harvey Oswald." McDonald claims to have finally tracked Saul down in London in 1972 at which time Saul revealed the details of the plot to him. ISBN 0-8217-3893-3.

See also

- *American Tabloid*, a 1995 novel by James Ellroy, which portrays the five years leading up to the assassination from the point of view of a group of Mafia associates and CIA operatives, who become embroiled in the Bay of Pigs Invasion and eventually help plan the crime.
- *The Cold Six Thousand*, a 2001 novel by James Ellroy, the sequel to *American Tabloid*. The first third of the novel portrays the cover-up the JFK assassination, while the remainder concerns the events leading up to the assassinations of Martin Luther King, Jr. and Robert F. Kennedy.
- *Executive Action*, a 1973 film by David Miller that portrays the assassination from the point of view of the conspirators, who are right-wing tycoons and former covert ops specialists.
- *JFK*, a 1991 film by Oliver Stone that portrays a somewhat fictionalized account of New Orleans District Attorney Jim Garrison's investigation into the assassination.
- Tikka to Ride, an episode of the British sci-fi sit-com *Red Dwarf*, deals with the assassination of John F. Kennedy, where, in a paradoxical turn of events, John himself turns out to be the "gunman behind the grassy knoll" in order to save the grim future of his country if he doesn't die.
- List of coups d'état and coup attempts

References

- Benson, Michael (2002). *Encyclopedia of The JFK Assassination*. Checkmark Books. ISBN 978-0816044771.
- Blakey, G. Robert (1981). *The Plot to Kill the President*. Crown Publishing Group. ISBN 13:9780812909296.
- Connally, Nellie; Herskowitz, Mickey (October 28, 2003). *From Love Field: Our Final Hours with President John F. Kennedy*. Rugged Land. ISBN 0-316-86032-8.
- Douglass, James W. (2008). *JFK and the Unspeakable: Why He Died and Why It Matters*. Orbis Books. ISBN 978-1570757556.
- Hancock, Larry (2006). *Someone Would Have Talked: The Assassination of President John F. Kennedy and the Conspiracy to Mislead History*. JFK Lancer Productions & Publications. ISBN 978-0977465712.

- Hurt, Henry. *Reasonable Doubt: An Investigation into the Assassination of John F. Kennedy.* New York: Holt, Rinehart and Winston, 1985. (ISBN 0-8050-0360-6)
- Kelin, John (2007). *Praise from a Future Generation: The Assassination of John F. Kennedy and the First Generation Critics of the Warren Report.* Wings Press. ISBN 978-0916727321.
- Lane, Mark (1966). *Rush to Judgment: A critique of the Warren Commission's inquiry in the murders of John F. Kennedy, Officer J.D. Tippit and Lee Harvey Oswald.* Holt, Rinehart and Winston. ISBN 978-0851360119.
- Marrs, Jim. *Crossfire: The Plot that Killed Kennedy*, New York: Carroll & Graf Publishers, 1989 (ISBN 0-88184-648-1).
- Newman, John M. (2008). *Oswald and the CIA: The Documented Truth Anout the Unknown Relationship Between the U.S. Government and the Alleged Killer of JFK.* Skyhorse Publishing. ISBN 978-1602392533.
- Michael Collins Piper. *Final Judgment: The Missing Link in the JFK Assassination Conspiracy*, America First Books, The American Free Press, 2005 (ISBN 0-9745484-0-5).
- Russell, Dick (2008). *On the Trail of the JFK Assassins: A Revealing Look at America's Most Infamous Unsolved Crime.* Skyhorse Publishing. ISBN 978-1602393226.
- Thompson, Josiah. *Six Seconds in Dallas: A Micro-Study of the Kennedy Assassination.* New York: Bernard Geis Associates, 1967. ISBN 978-0-394-44571-7
- Waldron, Lamar; Hartmann, Thom (2009). *Legacy of Secrecy: The Long Shadow of the JFK Assassination.* Counterpoint (Berkeley). ISBN 978-1-58243-535-0.
- *Who's Who in the JFK Assassination: An A-to-Z Encyclopedia* by Michael Benson Citadel Press, ISBN 0-8065-1444-2

External links

- The Kennedy Assassination Home Page by John McAdams [1]
- The Assassination of John F. Kennedy [2] — Index to articles on Spartacus Educational by John Simkin.
- Tech Puts JFK Conspiracy Theories to Rest [3] — Discovery article on a simulation that partially discredits some conspiracy theories
- Frontline: Who was L.H. Oswald [4] – PBS documentary on the man and his life
- PBS News 2003 [5] — Public's belief that a conspiracy existed
- "Oswald's Ghost" [4], an episode of PBS series *American Experience*, which aired January 14, 2008

Sirhan Sirhan

Sirhan Bishara Sirhan	
سرحان بشارة سرحان	
Sirhan Sirhan	
Born	Sirhan Bishara Sirhan March 19, 1944 Jerusalem, British Mandate of Palestine
Charge(s)	Assassination of Robert F. Kennedy
Penalty	Death, commuted to life imprisonment 1972
Status	Incarcerated
Parents	Bishara Sirhan and Mary Muzhea

Sirhan Bishara Sirhan (Arabic: سرحان بشارة سرحان, born March 19, 1944) is a Christian Palestinian (referred to as a Jordanian at the time of the assassination) who was convicted for the assassination of United States Senator Robert F. Kennedy. He is serving a life sentence at Pleasant Valley State Prison, California.

Personal information

Sirhan was born in Jerusalem to a Palestinian Christian family. When he was 12, his family emigrated, moving briefly to New York, and then to California. He attended Eliot Junior High School (now known as Charles W. Eliot Middle School) in Altadena, California, John Muir High School and Pasadena City College.[citation needed]

As an adult, he changed church denominations several times, joining Baptist and Seventh-day Adventist churches, and also dabbling in the occult. He was employed as a stable boy in 1965 at the Santa Anita race track in Arcadia, California.

Robert F. Kennedy assassination

Main article: Assassination of Robert F. Kennedy

On June 5, 1968, Sirhan fired a .22 caliber Iver-Johnson Cadet revolver at Senator Robert Kennedy and the crowd surrounding him in the Ambassador Hotel in Los Angeles shortly after Kennedy had finished addressing supporters in the hotel's main ballroom. George Plimpton, Rosey Grier, author Pete Hamill, and 1960 Olympic gold medalist Rafer Johnson were among several men who subdued and disarmed

Sirhan after a lengthy struggle.

Kennedy was shot three times, with a fourth bullet passing through his jacket, and died nearly 26 hours later. Five other people at the party were also shot, but all five recovered: Paul Schrade, an official with the United Automobile Workers union; William Weisel, an ABC TV unit manager; Ira Goldstein, a reporter with the Continental News Service; Elizabeth Evans, a friend of Pierre Salinger, one of Kennedy's campaign aides; and a teenager, Irwin Stroll, a Kennedy volunteer.

Prosecution

Despite Sirhan's admission of guilt, recorded in a confession made while in police custody on June 6, a lengthy trial followed. The court judge did not accept his confession and denied his request to withdraw his not guilty plea so that he could plead guilty. Sirhan later recanted his confession.

On February 10, 1969, a motion by Sirhan's lawyers to enter a plea of guilty to first degree murder in exchange for life imprisonment (rather than the death penalty) was made in chambers. Sirhan announced to the court judge, Herbert V. Walker, that he wanted to withdraw his original plea of not guilty in order to plead guilty as charged on all counts. He also asked that his counsel "...disassociate themselves from this case completely." When the judge asked him what he wanted to do about sentencing, Sirhan replied, "I will ask to be executed."

Judge Walker denied the motion and stated, "This court will not accept the plea..." The judge also denied Sirhan's request for his counsel to withdraw; when his counsel entered another motion to withdraw from the case of their own volition, Walker denied this motion as well. Judge Walker subsequently ordered that the record pertaining to the motion be sealed.

The trial proceeded, and opening statements began on February 12, 1969, a mere two days later. The lead prosecutor in the Sirhan case was Lynn "Buck" Compton, a WWII veteran (depicted in HBO's *Band of Brothers*) and now retired Justice of the California Court of Appeal. The prosecution's opening statement, delivered by David Fitts, was replete with examples of Sirhan's devious and deliberate preparations for murder. The prosecution was able to show that just two nights before the attack, on June 3, Sirhan was seen at the Ambassador Hotel, apparently attempting to learn the building's layout; evidence proved that he visited a gun range on June 4. Further testimony by Alvin Clark, Sirhan's garbage collector, who claimed that Sirhan had told him a month before the attack of his intention to shoot Kennedy, seemed especially damning.

Sirhan's Defense Counsel, which included Attorney Grant Cooper, had hoped to demonstrate that the killing had been an impulsive act of a man with a mental deficiency, but when Judge Walker admitted into evidence pages from three of the journal notebooks that Sirhan had kept, it was clear that the murder was not only premeditated, but also "...quite calculating and willful."

On March 3, 1969, in a Los Angeles courtroom, Cooper asked Sirhan point blank if he had indeed shot Senator Kennedy. Sirhan replied immediately: "Yes, Sir." but then stated that he did not bear any ill-will towards Kennedy. Sirhan also testified that he had killed Kennedy "with 20 years of malice aforethought," although he has maintained since being arrested that he has no memory of the crime.

During Sirhan's testimony, Cooper asked him to explain his reasons for the attack on Kennedy. Sirhan launched into "...a vicious diatribe about the Middle East conflict between Arab and Jew." Sirhan's anti-Zionist rhetoric was so passionate that one of his own defense counsel, Emile Zola Berman, who was Jewish, became upset and expressed his intentions to resign [yet again] from the defense team. Cooper eventually talked Berman out of resigning, who then stayed until the end of the trial.

During the trial, the defense primarily based their case on the expert testimony of Bernard L. Diamond M.D., a well known professor of law and psychiatry at University of California, Berkeley, who testified that Sirhan was suffering from diminished capacity at the time of the murder. Sirhan's behavior throughout the trial was indeed bizarre, and at one point, he became outraged during testimony about his childhood.

Sirhan was convicted on April 17, 1969, and was sentenced six days later to death in the gas chamber. Three years later, his sentence was commuted to life in prison, due to the California Supreme Court's decision in *People v. Anderson*, (*The People of the State of California v. Robert Page Anderson*, 493 P.2d 880, 6 Cal. 3d 628 (Cal. 1972)), which ruled capital punishment a violation of the California Constitution's prohibition of cruel or unusual punishment. The California Supreme Court declared in the Anderson case that its decision was retroactive, thereby invalidating all death sentences imposed in California.

Appeals

Sirhan's most recent lawyer, Lawrence Teeter later argued that Grant Cooper was compromised by a conflict of interest and was, as a consequence, grossly negligent in defense of his client. Other defense tactics included a motion for a new trial amid claims of set-ups, police bungles, hypnotism, brainwashing, blackmail, and government conspiracies. On June 5, 2003, coincidentally the 35th anniversary of Kennedy's assassination, Lawrence Teeter, petitioned a federal court in Los Angeles to move the case to Fresno. He stated that Sirhan would not get a fair hearing in Los Angeles, where a man who helped prosecute Sirhan is now a federal judge: U.S. District Judge William Matthew Byrne Jr. in Los Angeles was a deputy U.S. attorney during Sirhan's trial, and part of the prosecutorial team. Teeter, who had been trying since 1994 to have state and federal courts overturn the conviction, argued that his client was hypnotized and framed, possibly by a government conspiracy. He was granted a June 30 hearing. During the hearing, Teeter referenced testimony from the original trial transcripts regarding a prosecution eyewitness to the attack, author George Plimpton, in which he said that Sirhan looked "enormously composed. He seemed—purged." This statement coincided with the defense's argument that Sirhan had shot Kennedy while in some kind of hypnotic trance. The motion was denied.

Teeter died in 2005, and Sirhan declined other defense counsel to replace him.

Motives

A possible motive cited for his actions is the Middle East conflict. After his arrest, Sirhan said, "I can explain it. I did it for my country." According to Mel Ayton, Sirhan believed he was deliberately betrayed by Kennedy's support for Israel in the June 1967 Six-Day War, which had begun exactly one year to the day before the assassination. During a search of Sirhan's apartment after his arrest, a spiral-bound notebook was found containing a diary entry which demonstrated that his anger had gradually fixated on Robert Kennedy, who had promised to send 50 fighter jets to Israel if he were elected president. Sirhan's journal entry of May 18, 1968, read: "My determination to eliminate R.F.K. is becoming the more and more [sic] of an unshakable obsession...Kennedy must die before June 5th". They found other notebooks and diary entries which contained his growing rage at Zionists, particularly at Kennedy; his journals also contained many nonsensical scribbles, which were thought to be his version of "free writing".

The next day, on June 6, the *Los Angeles Times* printed an article, which discussed Sirhan's motive for the assassination, confirmed by the memos Sirhan wrote to himself. Jerry Cohen, who authored the article, stated,

> *"When the Jordanian nationalist, Sirhan Bishara Sirhan, allegedly shot Kennedy, ostensibly because of the senator's advocacy of U.S. support for Israel, the crime with which he was charged was in essence another manifestation of the centuries-old hatred between Arab and Jew."*

Dr. Mohammad Taki ("M. T.") Mehdi, then secretary-general of the Action Committee on American-Arab Relations, believed that Sirhan had acted in justifiable self-defense, stating: "Sirhan was defending himself against those 50 Phantom jets Kennedy was sending to Israel." Mehdi wrote a 100-page book on the subject called *"Kennedy and Sirhan: Why?"*.

Later in prison, Sirhan stated that his motivation was anger fueled by liquor. An interview with Sirhan in 1980 revealed new claims that a combination of liquor and anger over the anniversary of the 1967 Arab-Israeli war triggered his actions the night he assassinated RFK. "You must remember the circumstances of that night, June 5. That was when I was provoked," Sirhan says, recorded in a transcript of one of his interviews with Dr. Mehdi, now president of the New York-based American-Arab Relations Committee. "That is when I initially went to observe the Jewish Zionist parade in celebration of the June 5, 1967, victory over the Arabs. That was the catalyst that triggered me on that night." Then Sirhan said, "In addition, there was the consumption of the liquor, and I want the public to understand that..."

At a June 30, 2003 hearing, Lawrence Teeter, in an attempt to get Sirhan a new trial, claimed that Sirhan had been hypnotized into firing at Kennedy and that he may have been using blanks; that Sirhan couldn't possibly have fired the fatal shot from where he was standing; that prosecutors blackmailed his defense attorney to throw the case and that police and government agencies whitewashed or bungled investigations. The motion was denied.

Imprisonment

As of October 29, 2009, Sirhan is confined at Pleasant Valley State Prison in Coalinga, California, where he is housed in a cell by himself. From 1992 to 2009, Sirhan had been confined at the California State Prison (COR) in Corcoran, California and lived in COR's Protective Housing Unit until he was moved to a harsher lockdown at COR in 2003. Prior to 1992 he had been at the Correctional Training Facility (CTF) in Soledad, California.

Applications for parole

In a 1980 transcripted interview with M.T. Mehdi, Sirhan claimed his actions were fueled by liquor and anger. He then complained that the parole board was not taking these "mitigating" circumstances into account when they continually denied his parole.

On May 10, 1982, Sirhan told the parole board: "I sincerely believe that if Robert Kennedy were alive today, I believe he would not countenance singling me out for this kind of treatment. I think he would be among the first to say that, however horrible the deed I committed 14 years ago was, that it should not be the cause for denying me equal treatment under the laws of this country."

A parole hearing for Sirhan is now scheduled every five years. On March 15, 2006, he was denied parole for the 13th time. He did not attend the hearing, nor did he appoint a new attorney to represent him. His next possible chance for parole will be in 2011.

See also

- RFK (2002 film)
- RFK Must Die (2007 film)
- Bobby (2006 film)
- Sirhan Sirhan's notebook on WikiSource.org
- Notable Inmates at California State Prison, Corcoran
- Robert Kennedy in Palestine (1948)

Further reading

- Jansen, Godfrey, *Why Robert Kennedy Was Killed: The Story of Two Victims*, New York, Third Press, 1970. OCLC 137100 [1]
- Kaiser, Robert Blair, *"R.F.K. Must Die!": A History of the Robert Kennedy Assassination and Its Aftermath*, New York, E.P. Dutton & Co, Inc. 1970. ISBN 978-1-59020-070-4
- Kaiser, Robert Blair, *"R.F.K. Must Die!": Chasing the Mystery of the Robert Kennedy Assassination*, New York, Overlook Press, Peter Mayer Publishers, Inc. 2008. ISBN 978-1-59020-124-4

- Melanson, Philip H., *Who Killed Robert Kennedy?*, Berkeley, California, Odonian, 1993. ISBN 978-1-878825-12-4
- Turner, William V., and John G. Christian, *The Assassination of Robert F. Kennedy: A Searching Look at the Conspiracy and Cover-up 1968-1978*, New York, Random House, 1978. ISBN 978-0-394-40273-4
- Ayton, Mel, *The Forgotten Terrorist - Sirhan Sirhan and the Assassination of Robert F. Kennedy* Washington DC, Potomac Books, 2007. ISBN 978-1-59797-079-2
- Mehdi, Mohammad Taki, *Kennedy and Sirhan: Why?*, New World Press, 1968. Edition: Illustrated Paperback, 100 pages. ISBN 978-0-911026-04-7

External links

- Sirhan Sirhan [2] at the Internet Movie Database
- Crime Library biography [3]
- Interview with Sirhan's attorney Lawrence Teeter on KPFA 94.1 / Guns & Butter show [4]
- The Robert Kennedy Assassination - Statement [5]
- "The Robert Kennedy Assassination: Unraveling the Conspiracy Theories," [6] Mel Ayton, *Crime Magazine* May 8, 2005
- Los Angeles Daily Mirror story about Sirhan working as a delivery boy at a Pasadena health food store [7]

Assassination of Robert F. Kennedy

\multicolumn{2}{c}{**Robert F. Kennedy assassination**}
\multicolumn{2}{c}{Robert F. Kennedy}
Location	Ambassador Hotel, Los Angeles, California, USA
Date	June 5, 1968 12:15 a.m. (Pacific Time Zone)
Target	Robert F. Kennedy
Weapon(s)	.22 caliber Iver-Johnson
Death(s)	1
Injured	5
Belligerent	Sirhan Sirhan

The **assassination of Robert F. Kennedy**, a United States Senator and brother of assassinated President John F. Kennedy, took place shortly after midnight on June 5, 1968 in Los Angeles, California. After winning the California primary election for the Democratic nomination for President of the United States, Robert F. Kennedy was shot as he walked through the kitchen of the Ambassador Hotel and died in the Good Samaritan Hospital twenty-six hours later. Sirhan Sirhan, a twenty-four year old Palestinian immigrant, was convicted of Kennedy's murder and is serving a life sentence for the crime. The shooting was recorded on audio tape by a freelance newspaper reporter, and the aftermath was captured on film.

Kennedy's body lay in repose at St. Patrick's Cathedral in New York for two days before a funeral mass was held on June 8. His body was interred near his brother John at Arlington National Cemetery. His death prompted the protection of presidential candidates by the United States Secret Service. Hubert Humphrey went on to win the Democratic nomination for the presidency, but ultimately narrowly lost the election to Richard Nixon.

As with his brother's death, Robert Kennedy's assassination and the circumstances surrounding it have spawned a variety of conspiracy theories.

Background

Kennedy was United States Attorney General from January 1961 until September 3, 1964, when he resigned to run for election to the United States Senate. He took office as Senator from New York on January 3, 1965.

The approach of the 1968 presidential election saw the incumbent president, Lyndon B. Johnson, serving during a period of social unrest. There were riots in the major cities despite Johnson's attempts to introduce anti-poverty and anti-discrimination legislation, and there was significant opposition to the ongoing military action in Vietnam. The assassination of Martin Luther King, Jr. in April 1968 led to further riots in 100 cities. Kennedy entered the race for the Democratic Party's nomination for president on March 16, 1968—four days after Senator Eugene McCarthy received a large percentage of the vote in the New Hampshire primary against the incumbent President (42% to Johnson's 49%). Two weeks later, a demoralized Johnson announced he was no longer seeking re-election. One month later, Vice President Hubert Humphrey announced he would seek the presidency. Humphrey did not participate in any primaries but he did obtain the support of many Democratic Party delegates. Following the California primary, Kennedy was in second place with 393 delegates compared to Humphrey's 561.

Assassination

Four hours after the polls closed in California, Kennedy claimed victory in the state's Democratic presidential primary. At approximately 12:15 a.m. PDT, he addressed his campaign supporters in the Ambassador Hotel's Embassy Room ballroom, in the Mid-Wilshire district of Los Angeles. At the time, the government provided Secret Service protection for incumbent presidents but not for presidential candidates. Kennedy's only security was provided by former FBI agent William Barry and two unofficial bodyguards, former professional athletes. During the campaign, Kennedy had welcomed contact with the public, and people had often tried to touch him in their excitement.

Kennedy had planned to walk through the ballroom when he had finished speaking, on his way to another gathering of supporters elsewhere in the hotel. However, with deadlines fast approaching, reporters wanted a press conference. Campaign aide Fred Dutton decided that Kennedy would forgo the second gathering and instead go through the kitchen and pantry area behind the ballroom to the press area. Kennedy finished speaking and started to exit when William Barry stopped him and said, "No, it's been changed. We're going this way." Barry and Dutton began clearing a way for Kennedy to go left through swinging doors to the kitchen corridor, but Kennedy, hemmed in by the crowd, followed hotel maître d' Karl Uecker through a back exit.

Uecker led Kennedy through the kitchen area, holding Kennedy's right wrist but frequently releasing it as Kennedy shook hands with those he encountered. Uecker and Kennedy started down a passageway narrowed by an ice machine against the right wall and a steam table to the left. Kennedy turned to his left and shook hands with busboy Juan Romero as Sirhan Sirhan stepped down from a low tray-stacker beside the ice machine, rushed past Uecker, and repeatedly fired what was later identified as a .22 caliber Iver-Johnson Cadet revolver.

After Kennedy had fallen to the floor, security man Bill Barry hit Sirhan twice in the face while others, including maître d's Uecker and Edward Minasian, writer George Plimpton, Olympic gold medal decathlete Rafer Johnson and professional football player Rosey Grier, forced Sirhan against the steam table and disarmed him. Sirhan wrestled free and grabbed the revolver again, but he had already fired all the bullets. Barry went to Kennedy and laid his jacket under the candidate's head, later recalling: "I knew immediately it was a .22, a small caliber, so I hoped it wouldn't be so bad, but then I saw the hole in the Senator's head, and I knew". Reporters and photographers rushed into the area from both directions, contributing to the chaos. As Kennedy lay wounded, Juan Romero cradled the senator's head and placed a rosary in his hand. Kennedy asked Romero, "Is everybody safe, OK?" and Romero responded, "Yes, yes, everything is going to be OK". Captured by *Life* photographer Bill Eppridge and Boris Yaro of the *Los Angeles Times*, this moment became the iconic image of the assassination.

Ethel Kennedy stood outside the crush of people at the scene, seeking help. She was soon led to her husband and knelt beside him. He turned his head and seemed to recognize her. After several minutes, medical attendants arrived and lifted Kennedy onto a stretcher, prompting him to whisper, "Don't lift me". He lost consciousness shortly thereafter. Kennedy was taken a mile away to Central Receiving Hospital, where he arrived near death. One doctor slapped his face, calling, "Bob, Bob", while another massaged Kennedy's heart. After obtaining a good heartbeat, doctors handed a stethoscope to Ethel Kennedy so she could hear her husband's heart beating, much to her relief. After about 30 minutes, Kennedy was transferred several blocks to the Hospital of the Good Samaritan for surgery. Surgery began at 3:12 a.m. PDT and lasted three hours and 40 minutes. Ten and a half hours later, at 5:30 p.m. PDT on Wednesday, spokesman Frank Mankiewicz announced that Kennedy's doctors were "concerned over his continuing failure to show improvement"; his condition remained "extremely critical as to life".

Kennedy had been shot three times. One bullet, fired at a range of about 1 inch (2.54 cm), entered behind his right ear, dispersing fragments throughout his brain. Two others entered at the rear of his right armpit; one exited from his chest and the other lodged in the back of his neck. Despite extensive neurosurgery at the Good Samaritan Hospital to remove the bullet and bone fragments from his brain, Kennedy died at 1:44 a.m. PDT on June 6, nearly 26 hours after the shooting. Five other people were also wounded: William Weisel of ABC News, Paul Schrade of the United Auto Workers union, Democratic Party activist Elizabeth Evans, Ira Goldstein of the Continental News Service and Kennedy campaign volunteer Irwin Stroll. Although not physically wounded, singer Rosemary Clooney, a strong Kennedy supporter, was present in the ballroom during the shooting in the pantry and suffered a nervous breakdown shortly afterward.

Sirhan Sirhan

Main article: Sirhan Sirhan

Sirhan Sirhan was strongly anti-Zionist. A diary found during a search of Sirhan's home stated, "My determination to eliminate RFK is becoming more and more of an unshakable obsession. RFK must die. RFK must be killed. Robert F. Kennedy must be assassinated...Robert F. Kennedy must be assassinated before 5 June 68." It has been suggested that the date of the assassination is significant, because it was the first anniversary of the first day of the Six Day War between Israel and its Arab neighbors. When Sirhan was booked by police, they found in his pocket a newspaper article that discussed Kennedy's support for Israel, and at his trial, Sirhan testified that he began to hate Kennedy after learning of this support. This interpretation of his motives has, however, been criticized as an oversimplification that ignores Sirhan's deeper psychological problems.

During his trial, Sirhan's lawyers attempted to use a defense of diminished responsibility, while their client tried to confess to the crime and change his plea to guilty on several occasions. Sirhan testified that he had killed Kennedy "with 20 years of malice aforethought", although he has maintained since being convicted that he has no memory of the crime. The judge did not accept this confession and it was later withdrawn.

Sirhan was convicted on April 17, 1969, and six days later was sentenced to death. The sentence was commuted to life in prison in 1972 after the California Supreme Court, in its decision in *California v. Anderson*, invalidated all pending death sentences imposed in California prior to 1972. In 2006, he was denied parole for the thirteenth time and is currently confined at the Pleasant Valley State Prison in Coalinga, CA.

Media coverage

As the shooting took place, ABC News was signing off from its electoral broadcast, while the CBS broadcast was already over. It was not until 21 minutes after the shots that CBS's coverage of the shooting would begin. The reporters who had been present to report on Kennedy's win in the primary ended up crowding into the kitchen where he had been shot and the immediate aftermath was captured only by audio recording and cameras that had no live transmission capability. ABC was able to show scant live footage from the kitchen after Kennedy had been transported but unlike CBS and NBC, all of ABC's coverage from the Ambassador was in black and white. CBS and NBC shot footage in the kitchen of the shooting's aftermath on color film, which could not be broadcast until it was developed two hours after the incident.

Reporter Andrew West of KRKD, a Mutual Broadcasting System radio affiliate in Los Angeles, captured on audio tape the sounds of the immediate aftermath of the shooting but not the actual shooting itself. Using a reel-to-reel tape recorder and attached microphone, West also provided an on-the-spot account of the struggle with Sirhan in the hotel kitchen pantry, shouting at Rafer Johnson to

"Get the gun, Rafer, get the gun!" and telling others to "get a hold of [Sirhan's] thumb and break it, if you have to! Get his thumb!"Wikipedia:Link rot

Over the following week, NBC devoted 55 hours to the shooting and aftermath, ABC 43, and CBS 42, with all three networks preempting their regular coverage and advertisements to cover the story.

Conspiracy theories

Main article: Robert F. Kennedy assassination conspiracy theories

As with the assassination of President John F. Kennedy, Robert Kennedy's brother, in 1963, the senator's death has been the subject of widespread analysis. Some individuals involved in the original investigation and some researchers have suggested alternative scenarios for the crime, or have argued that there are serious problems with the official case.

CIA involvement theory

In November 2006, the BBC's *Newsnight* program presented research by filmmaker Shane O'Sullivan alleging that several CIA officers were present on the night of the assassination. Three men who appear in films and photographs from the night of the assassination were positively identified by former colleagues and associates as former senior CIA officers who had worked together in 1963 at JMWAVE, the CIA's main anti-Castro station based in Miami. They were JMWAVE Chief of Operations David Morales, Chief of Maritime Operations Gordon Campbell and Chief of Psychological Warfare Operations George Joannides.

The program featured an interview with Morales's former attorney Robert Walton, who quoted him as having said, "I was in Dallas when we got the son of a bitch and I was in Los Angeles when we got the little bastard". O'Sullivan reported that the CIA declined to comment on the officers in question. It was also alleged that Morales was known for his deep anger toward the Kennedys for what he saw as their betrayal during the Bay of Pigs Invasion.

After further investigation, O'Sullivan produced the feature documentary, *RFK Must Die*. The film casts doubt on the earlier identifications and ultimately reveals that the man previously identified as Gordon Campbell may, in fact, have been Michael D. Roman, a now-deceased Bulova Watch Company employee, who was at the Ambassador Hotel for a company convention.

Second gunman theory

The location of Kennedy's wounds suggested that his assailant had stood behind him, but some witnesses said that Sirhan faced west as Kennedy moved through the pantry facing east. This has led to the suggestion that a second gunman actually fired the fatal shot, a possibility supported by coroner Thomas Noguchi who stated that the fatal shot was behind Kennedy's right ear and had been fired at a distance of approximately one inch. Other witnesses, though, said that as Sirhan approached, Kennedy was turning to his left shaking hands, facing north and so exposing his right side. As recently as 2008, eyewitness John Pilger asserted his belief that there must have been a second gunman. During a re-examination of the case in 1975, the Los Angeles Superior Court ordered expert examination of the possibility of a second gun having been used, and the conclusion of the experts was that there was little or no evidence to support this theory.

In 2007, analysis of an audio tape recording of the shooting made by freelance reporter Stanislaw Pruszynski appeared to indicate, according to forensic expert Philip Van Praag, that thirteen shots were fired, even though Sirhan's gun held only eight rounds. Van Praag states that the recording also reveals at least two cases where the timing between shots was shorter than humanly possible. The presence of more than eight shots on the tape was corroborated by forensic audio specialists Wes Dooley and Paul Pegas of Audio Engineering Associates in Pasadena, California, forensic audio and ballistics expert Eddy B. Brixen in Copenhagen, Denmark, and audio specialist Phil Spencer Whitehead of the Georgia Institute of Technology in Atlanta, Georgia. Some other acoustic experts, however, have stated that no more than eight shots were recorded on the audio tape.

Aftermath and legacy

Memorial

Following the autopsy on June 6, Kennedy's body was returned to New York City, where he lay in repose at St. Patrick's Cathedral, viewed by thousands, until a funeral mass on the morning of June 8.

Kennedy's younger brother, U.S. Senator Edward "Ted" Kennedy, eulogized him with the words:

> My brother need not be idealized, or enlarged in death beyond what he was in life; to be remembered simply as a good and decent man, who saw wrong and tried to right it, saw suffering and tried to heal it, saw war and tried to stop it. Those of us who loved him and who take him to his rest today, pray that what he was to us and what he wished for others will some day come to pass for all the world. As he said many times, in many parts of this nation, to those he touched and who sought to touch him: 'Some men see things as they are and say why. I dream things that never were and say why not.'

Robert Kennedy's Grave in Arlington National Cemetery

Immediately following the mass, Kennedy's body was transported by a slow-moving train to Washington, D.C. and thousands of mourners lined the tracks and stations, paying their respects as the train passed by. Kennedy was buried near his older brother John, in Arlington National Cemetery, in the first burial ever to take place there at night; the second being the burial of his younger brother Ted.

After the assassination, Congress altered the Secret Service's mandate to include protection for presidential candidates. The remaining candidates were immediately protected under an executive order issued by Lyndon Johnson, putting a strain on the poorly resourced Secret Service.

1968 election

At the time of his death, Kennedy was significantly behind Humphrey in convention delegate support, but many believe that Kennedy would have ultimately secured the nomination following his victory in the California primary. Only thirteen states held primaries that year, meaning that most delegates at the Democratic convention could choose a candidate based on their personal preference.Wikipedia:Link rot Historian Arthur M. Schlesinger, Jr. and others have argued that Kennedy's broad appeal and charisma would have been sufficiently convincing at the 1968 Democratic National Convention to give him the nomination. Historian Michael Beschloss believed, however, that Kennedy would not have secured the nomination. Humphrey, after a National Convention in Chicago marred by violence in the streets, was far behind in opinion polls but gained ground. He ultimately lost the general election to Republican Richard Nixon by a narrow margin.

See also

- *Bobby* (2006 film)
- Kennedy Curse
- Kennedy family
- List of assassinated American politicians

References

Bibliography

- Coleman, Loren (2004). *The Copycat Effect: How the Media and Popular Culture Trigger the Mayhem in Tomorrow's Headlines*. New York: Paraview Pocket. ISBN 978-0743482233.
- Moldea, Dan E. (1995). *The Killing of Robert F. Kennedy: An Investigation of Motive, Means, and Opportunity*. New York: Norton. ISBN 978-0393037913.
- Schlesinger, Jr., Arthur M. (1996). *Robert Kennedy and His Times*. Ballantine Books. ISBN 0345410610.
- Noguchi, Thomas (1985). *Coroner*. New York: Simon & Schuster. ISBN 978-0671467722.
- Thomas, Evan (2000). *Robert Kennedy: His Life*. New York: Simon & Schuster. ISBN 978-0684834801.
- Witcover, Jules (1969). *85 Days: The Last Campaign of Robert Kennedy*. New York: Putnam. OCLC 452367 [1].

Further reading

Two Minutes to Midnight: The Very Last Hurrah [2] Account of the assassination and observations by Pete Hamill for the Village Voice June 13, 1968

External links

- Mary Ferrell Foundation - RFK Assassination Documents [3] – LAPD and FBI investigation files and the trial transcript at the Mary Ferrell Foundation

Geographical coordinates: 34°03'35"N 118°17'50"W

Modern Failed Attempts

Lynette Fromme

Lynette Fromme	
Born	October 22, 1948 Santa Monica, California, US
Charge(s)	Attempted assassination of a US President
Penalty	Life in prison
Status	Paroled
Parents	William Millar Fromme Helen Benzinger

Lynette Alice "Squeaky" Fromme (born October 22, 1948) is an American member of the Manson Family. She was sentenced to life imprisonment for attempting to assassinate U.S. President Gerald Ford in 1975. After serving 34 years in custody, she was released from prison on August 14, 2009.

Early life

Fromme was born in Santa Monica, California, the daughter of William Millar Fromme, an aeronautical engineer, and Helen Benzinger, a homemaker.

As a child, Fromme was a performer for a popular local dance group called the Westchester Lariats, which in the late 1950s began touring the U.S. and Europe, appearing on *The Lawrence Welk Show* and at the White House. Fromme was in the 1959 tour.

In 1963, the family moved to Redondo Beach, a suburb of Los Angeles, in the South Bay, and Fromme began drinking and taking drugs. Her grades at Redondo Union High School dropped, but she managed to graduate in 1966. She moved out of her parents' house for a few months before her father convinced her to consider El Camino Junior College. Her attendance there only lasted about two months before an argument with her father rendered her homeless.

Charles Manson and Manson Family involvement

In 1967, Fromme went to Venice Beach, suffering from depression. Charles Manson, who had been recently released from federal prison at Terminal Island, between San Pedro and Long Beach, saw her and struck up a conversation. Fromme found Manson's philosophies and attitudes appealing, and the two became friends, traveling together and with other young people such as Mary Brunner and Susan Atkins. She lived in Southern California at Spahn Ranch, and in the desert near Death Valley.

After Manson and some of his followers were arrested for the Tate/La Bianca murders in 1969, Fromme and the remaining "Manson family" camped outside of the trial. When Manson and his fellow defendants, Patricia Krenwinkel, Leslie Van Houten and Atkins carved Xs into their foreheads, so did Fromme and her compatriots. They proclaimed Manson's innocence and preached his apocalyptic philosophy to the news media and to anyone else who would listen. She was never charged with involvement in the murders, but was convicted of attempting to prevent Manson's imprisoned followers from testifying, as well as contempt of court when she herself refused to testify. She was given short jail sentences for both offenses.

Upon entering prison, Charles Manson looked to the Aryan Brotherhood for protection against sexual assault and beatings. To earn the favor of the brotherhood, Manson had his female followers mail nude photos of themselves to brotherhood members. With these photos, promises of sexual favors when the men were released were also included.

Murder in Stockton, California

To follow through with Manson's deal with the Aryan Brotherhood, Fromme moved to Stockton, California, with friends Nancy Pitman and Priscilla Cooper, and a pair of ex-convict Aryan Brotherhood members named Michael Monfort and James Craig. This group happened to meet up with a couple, James and Lauren Willett, at a cabin. The ex-convicts forced James Willett to dig his own grave and gunned him down because he was going to tell the authorities about a series of robberies that the ex-convicts had committed after they were released from prison. After the body of James Willett was found, with his hand still sticking from the ground, the housemates were taken into custody on suspicion of murder. After their arrest, the body of Lauren Willett was discovered as well. An infant girl believed to be the Willetts' daughter was also found in the house in Stockton, and placed with Mary Graham Hall. Fromme was released due to a lack of evidence.

The Sonoma County coroner's office concluded that James Willett was killed sometime in September 1972 although his body was not found until the beginning of November 1972. He had been buried near Guerneville in Sonoma County. On the night of Saturday November 11, 1972 the Stockton Police responded to information that a station wagon owned by the Willetts was in the area. It was discovered parked in front of 720 W. Flora Street. "Police Sgt. Richard Whiteman went to the house and, when he was refused entry, forced his way in. All the persons subsequently arrested were in the house except for

Miss Fromme. She telephoned the house while police were there, asking to be picked up, and officers obliged, taking her into custody nearby. Police found a quantity of guns and ammunition in the house along with amounts of marijuana, and noticed freshly dug earth beneath the building."

The Stockton Police obtained a warrant and dug up the body of Lauren Willett around 5 a.m. the following day. Cooper told investigators that Lauren had been shot accidentally and had been buried when they realized she was dead. Cooper contended that Monfort was "demonstrating the dangers of firearms, playing a form of Russian roulette with a .38 caliber pistol" and had first spun the gun cylinder and shot at his own head, and when the gun didn't fire, pointed it at the victim, whereupon it fired. The Stockton Police indicated that Lauren Willett "was with the others of her own volition prior to the shooting, and was not being held prisoner."

Fromme was held in custody for two and a half months but never charged. The other four people involved were convicted. In an interview from the San Joaquin County Jail, she told reporters that she had been traveling in California trying to visit "brothers" in jail and to visit Manson. Fromme said that she came to Stockton to visit William Goucher, who was already in jail on a robbery charge when Mrs. Willett died. She claimed to be innocent of any wrongdoing. "They told me I was being put in here for murder because I didn't have anything to say." She also said from jail, "I know there's lots of people who've spent time for being quiet. That's why Charlie is in jail."

Fromme stated that she took a bus from Los Angeles to Stockton on Friday November 10, 1972, to visit Goucher whom she described as "a brother". She called Pittman, she said, and spent Friday night at the Flora Street house. When she left the jail after visiting Goucher Saturday, she called the house "to ask someone to pick me up". Stockton Police traced the call and arrested her at a phone booth.

After leaving Stockton, Fromme moved into a Sacramento apartment with fellow Manson family member Sandra Good. The two wore robes on occasion and changed their names to symbolize their devotion to Manson's new religion, Fromme becoming "Red" in honor of her red hair and the redwoods, and Good, "Blue", for her blue eyes and the ocean; both nicknames were originally given them by Manson.

Attempt to contact Jimmy Page

During Led Zeppelin's North American concert tour in 1975, Fromme contacted the band's publicist Danny Goldberg before a performance at the Long Beach Arena asking to meet with guitarist Jimmy Page. Fromme claimed to have foreseen the future and wished to forewarn Page of the imminent danger. Goldberg agreed to deliver the message if she were to commit it to writing. Allegedly, the note was burnt.

Assassination attempt on President Ford

On the morning of September 5, 1975, Fromme went to Sacramento's Capitol Park (reportedly to plead with President Gerald Ford about the plight of the California redwoods) dressed in a nun-like red robe and armed with a M1911A1.45 Colt semi-automatic pistol that she pointed at Ford. The pistol's magazine was loaded with four rounds, but none were in the firing chamber. She was immediately restrained by Larry Buendorf, a Secret Service agent. While being further restrained and handcuffed, Fromme managed to say a few sentences to the on-scene cameras, emphasizing that the gun "didn't go off". Fromme subsequently told *The Sacramento Bee* that she had deliberately ejected the cartridge in her weapon's chamber before leaving home that morning, and investigators later found a .45 ACP cartridge in her bathroom.

After a lengthy trial in which she refused to cooperate with her own defense, she was convicted of the attempted assassination of the president and received a life sentence under a 1965 law, prompted by the assassination of President John F. Kennedy, which made attempted presidential assassinations a federal crime punishable by a maximum sentence of life in prison. When U.S. Attorney Duane Keyes recommended severe punishment because she was "full of hate and violence," Fromme threw an apple at him, hitting him in the face and knocking off his glasses.

"I stood up and waved a gun (at Ford) for a reason," said Fromme. "I was so relieved not to have to shoot it, but, in truth, I came to get life. Not just my life but clean air, healthy water and respect for creatures and creation."

Aftermath

Seventeen days after Fromme's arrest, Sara Jane Moore attempted to assassinate Ford outside the St. Francis Hotel in San Francisco. Moore was quickly restrained by a bystander named Oliver Sipple, a decorated veteran, and the single shot fired from her gun slightly injured a taxi driver named John Ludwig who happened to be standing inside the hotel.

In 1979, Fromme was transferred out of the women's prison in Dublin, California, for attacking a fellow inmate, Julienne Busic, with the claw end of a hammer. On December 23, 1987, she escaped from the Alderson Federal Prison Camp in Alderson, West Virginia, attempting to meet up with Manson, whom she had heard had testicular cancer. She was captured again two days later and incarcerated at the Federal Medical Center, Carswell in Fort Worth, Texas.

Fromme first became eligible for parole in 1985, and was entitled by federal law to a mandatory hearing after 30 years but could waive that hearing and apply for release at a later date. Fromme steadfastly waived her right to request a hearing and was required by federal law to complete a parole application before one could be considered and granted. Fromme was granted parole in July 2008, but was not released due to the extra time added to her sentence for the 1987 prison escape.

Fromme, Federal Bureau of Prisons#06075-180, was released on parole from Federal Medical Center, Carswell on August 14, 2009. She then reportedly moved to Marcy, New York.

In media

Lynette Fromme's story is one of nine told in Stephen Sondheim and John Weidman's musical *Assassins*. She and John Hinckley, Jr. appear in the duet "Unworthy of Your Love".

Bibliography

- Bravin, Jess (1997). *Squeaky: The Life and Times Of Lynette Alice Fromme*. St. Martin's Press. ISBN 0312187629.

External links

- Federal BOP Inmate Locator showing Fromme's current status [1]

Sara Jane Moore

Sara Jane Moore	
Born	February 15, 1930 Charleston, West Virginia, U.S.
Charge(s)	Attempted assassination of a U.S. President
Penalty	Life sentence
Status	On parole

Sara Jane Moore (born **Sara Jane Kahn** on February 15, 1930) attempted to assassinate U.S. President Gerald Ford on September 22, 1975, outside the St. Francis Hotel in San Francisco, just seventeen days after Lynette "Squeaky" Fromme had pointed a gun at the president.

Background

A native of Charleston, West Virginia, she was a former nursing school student, Women's Army Corps recruit, and accountant. Moore had married and divorced five times and had four children before she turned to revolutionary politics in 1975.

Moore's friends said she had a deep fascination and obsession with Patty Hearst. After Hearst was kidnapped by the Symbionese Liberation Army, her father Randolph Hearst created the organization People in Need (P.I.N.) to feed the poor, in order to answer S.L.A. claims that the elder Hearst was "committing 'crimes' against 'the people.'" Moore was a bookkeeper for P.I.N. and an FBI informant when she attempted to assassinate Ford.

Attempted assassination of Gerald Ford

Moore had been evaluated by the Secret Service earlier in 1975, but that organization had decided that she presented no danger to the President. She had been picked up by police on an illegal handgun charge the day before the Ford incident, but was released from arrest. The police confiscated her .44 caliber pistol and 113 rounds of pistol ammunition.

Moore was about 40 feet away from President Ford when she fired a single shot at him with a different pistol, a .38 caliber revolver. Sara Jane was standing in the crowd across the street

Reaction approximately one second after the assassination attempt.

from the St. Francis Hotel. She was using a gun she bought in haste that same morning and did not know the sight was off by six inches. When she fired at Ford, her bullet just missed his head by a mere six inches. FBI case agent, Richard Vitamanti, measured the location the next day. After she fired her first shot and realized she had missed, she raised her arm again, and Oliver Sipple, a Marine, dove towards her, knocking her arm the second time, and saving President Ford's life. Judge Samuel Conti, still on the bench in 2010, spoke on the record, that Moore would have killed President Ford had she had her own gun, and it was only "because her gun was faulty," that saved the president's life. (Geri Spieler, author of "Taking Aim At The President," Palgrave Macmillan, Jan. 2009.) That bullet missed the President because a bystander, Oliver Sipple, grabbed Moore's arm and then pulled her to the ground, using his hand to keep the pistol from firing a second time. Sipple said at the time: "I saw [her gun] pointed out there and I grabbed for it. [...] I lunged and grabbed the woman's arm and the gun went off." The single shot which Moore did fire from her .38 caliber revolver ricocheted off the entrance to the hotel and it slightly injured a bystander.

Trial and imprisonment

Moore pleaded guilty to attempted assassination and was sentenced to life in prison. At her sentencing hearing Moore stated: "Am I sorry I tried? Yes and no. Yes, because it accomplished little except to throw away the rest of my life. And, no, I'm not sorry I tried, because at the time it seemed a correct expression of my anger."

In 1979, Moore escaped from the Alderson Federal Prison Camp in Alderson, West Virginia, but was recaptured only hours later. After her return, she was transferred to a more secure facility, and she served the remainder of her term at the federal women's prison in Dublin, California.

In an interview in 2004, former President Ford described Moore as "off her mind" and said that he continued making public appearances, even after two attempts on his life within such a short time, because "a president has to be aggressive, has to meet the people."

Moore had the Federal Bureau of Prisons register number 04851-180.

Release

On December 31, 2007, at the age of 77, Moore was released from prison on parole after serving 32 years of her life sentence. Ford had died from natural causes on December 26, 2006, one year and five days before her release. Moore has stated that she regrets the assassination attempt, saying she was "blinded by her radical political views." She will be under supervised parole for at least five years. Moore was released under a federal law that makes parole mandatory for inmates who have served at least 30 years of a life sentence and have maintained a satisfactory disciplinary record. When asked about her crime in an interview, Moore stated, "I am very glad I did not succeed. I know now that I was wrong to try."

Today Show

On May 28, 2009, Moore appeared on NBC's *Today* program, her first television appearance since leaving prison on parole. She told anchorman Matt Lauer, "I am glad that I didn't kill [Ford], but I don't regret trying."

Moore also discussed her 1979 escape from prison. She revealed that an inmate told her, "...when jumping the fence just put your hand on the barbed wire, you'll only have a few puncture wounds." She went on to say, "If I knew that I was going to be captured several hours later, I would have stopped at the local bar to get a drink or at a burger place just to get a drink and a burger."

Quotes

- "I do regret I didn't succeed, and allow the winds of change to start. I wish I had killed him. I did it to create chaos."
- "I didn't want to kill anybody, but there comes a point when the only way you can make a statement is to pick up a gun."
- "The government had declared war on the left. Nixon's appointment of Ford as vice president and his resignation making Ford president seemed to be a continuing assault on America."
- "I know now that I was wrong to try. Thank God I didn't succeed. People kept saying he would have to die before I could be released, and I did not want my release from prison to be dependent on somebody, on something happening to somebody else, so I wanted him to live to be 100."

External links

- Photograph of both Sipple and Moore taken during the assassination attempt; the black arrow points to Moore. [1]
- Photograph of Ford and his Secret Service agents taken just after Moore fired her shot. [2]
- Photographs of both the Fromme and Moore assassination attempts from the Ford Presidential Library. [3]
- More photographs of both the Fromme and Moore assassination attempts from the Ford Presidential Library. [4]
- Federal BOP Inmate Locator showing Sara Moore's current status [5]

John Hinckley, Jr.

John W. Hinckley, Jr.	
Born	John Warnock Hinckley, Jr. May 29, 1955 Ardmore, Oklahoma
Parents	John Warnock Hinckley, Sr., and Jo Ann Moore

John Warnock Hinckley, Jr., (born May 29, 1955) attempted to assassinate U.S. President Ronald Reagan in Washington, D.C., on March 30, 1981, as the culmination of an effort to impress actress Jodie Foster. He was found not guilty by reason of insanity and has remained under institutional psychiatric care since then. Public outcry over the verdict led to the Insanity Defense Reform Act of 1984.

Early life

John W. Hinckley, Jr., was born in Ardmore, Oklahoma. His father was John Warnock Hinckley, Sr., who was president of World Vision, and his mother was Jo Ann Moore Hinckley. He has two siblings – sister Diane and brother Scott. Hinckley grew up in University Park, Texas and attended Highland Park High School in Dallas County, Texas. The family, owners of the Hinckley Oil company, later settled in Evergreen, Colorado. Hinckley graduated in 1973 from high school in Texas which prompted the move to Evergreen, Colorado (Hansell & Damour, 2005). An off-and-on student at Texas Tech University from 1974 to 1980, in 1975 he headed to Los Angeles in the hope of becoming a songwriter. These efforts were unsuccessful, and his letters home to his parents were full of tales of misfortune and pleas for money. He also spoke of a girlfriend, Lynn Collins, who turned out to be a fabrication. He returned to his parents' home in Evergreen before the year was out. During the next few years, he developed a pattern of living on his own for a while and then returning home poor.

Obsession with Jodie Foster

Hinckley watched the 1976 movie *Taxi Driver* on a continuous loop in which a disturbed protagonist, Travis Bickle, played by Robert De Niro, plots to assassinate a presidential candidate. Hinckley developed an obsession with actress Jodie Foster, who had played a child prostitute in the film. The Bickle character was in turn partially based on the diaries of Arthur Bremer, the attempted assassin of George Wallace. When Foster entered Yale University, Hinckley moved to New Haven, Connecticut for a short time to stalk her, slipping poems and messages under her door and repeatedly contacting her by telephone.

Failing to develop any meaningful contact with Foster, Hinckley developed such plots as hijacking an airplane and committing suicide in front of her to gain her attention. Eventually he settled on a scheme to win her over by assassinating the president, with the theory that as a historical figure he would be her equal. To this end, he trailed President Jimmy Carter from state to state, but was arrested in Nashville, Tennessee on a firearms charge. Penniless, he returned home once again, and despite psychiatric treatment for depression, his mental health did not improve. He began to target newly-elected President Ronald Reagan in 1981. It was also at this time that he started collecting information on the assassination of John F. Kennedy by Lee Harvey Oswald, whom he saw as a role model.

Hinckley wrote to Foster just before his attempt on Reagan's life:

> Over the past seven months I've left you dozens of poems, letters and love messages in the faint hope that you could develop an interest in me. Although we talked on the phone a couple of times I never had the nerve to simply approach you and introduce myself. [...] the reason I'm going ahead with this attempt now is because I cannot wait any longer to impress you.

Assassination attempt

Main article: Reagan assassination attempt

On March 30, 1981, Hinckley fired a .22 caliber Röhm RG-14 revolver six times at Reagan as he left the Hilton Hotel in Washington, D.C., after addressing an AFL-CIO conference.

Hinckley wounded press secretary James Brady, police officer Thomas Delahanty, and Secret Service agent Timothy McCarthy. Hinckley did not directly hit Reagan, but seriously wounded him when a bullet ricocheted off the side of the presidential limousine and hit him in the chest. Hinckley did not attempt to flee and was arrested at the scene. All of the shooting victims survived, although Brady, who was hit in the right side of the head, endured a long recuperation period and remained paralyzed on the left side of his body.

Crowds outside the Washington Hilton Hotel after the assassination attempt on President Reagan.

Bush-Hinckley family connections

According to the March 31, 1981, edition of the *Houston Post*, and reported by AP, UPI, NBC News and *Newsweek*, Hinckley is the son of one of George H.W. Bush's political and financial supporters in his 1980 presidential primary campaign against Ronald Reagan; John Hinckley, Jr.'s elder brother, Scott Hinckley, and Bush's son Neil Bush had a dinner appointment scheduled for the next day.

Associated Press published the following on March 31, 1981:

> The family of the man charged with trying to assassinate President Reagan is acquainted with the family of Vice-President George Bush and had made large contributions to his political campaign ... Scott Hinckley, brother of John W. Hinckley, Jr., was to have dined tonight in Denver at the home of Neil Bush, one of the Vice-President's sons ... The Houston Post said it was unable to reach Scott Hinckley, vice-president of his father's Denver-based firm, Vanderbilt Energy Corporation, for comment. Neil Bush lives in Denver, where he works for Standard Oil Company of Indiana. In 1978, Neil Bush served as campaign manager for his brother, George W. Bush, the Vice-President's eldest son, who made an unsuccessful bid for Congress. Neil lived in Lubbock, Texas, throughout much of 1978, where John Hinckley lived from 1974 through 1980.

Trial

At the trial in 1982, charged with 13 offences, Hinckley was found not guilty by reason of insanity on June 21. The defense psychiatric reports found him to be insane while the prosecution reports declared him legally sane. Hinckley was confined at St. Elizabeths Hospital in Washington, D.C.

Hinckley, Federal Bureau of Prisons (BOP) # 00137-177, was released from BOP custody on August 18, 1981.

Reaction to verdict

The verdict led to widespread dismay; as a result, the U.S. Congress and a number of states rewrote laws regarding the insanity defense. Idaho, Montana, and Utah have abolished the defense altogether. In the United States prior to the Hinckley case, the insanity defense had been used in less than 2% of all felony cases and was unsuccessful in almost 75% of the trials in which it was used. Hinckley's parents wrote a book in 1985, *Breaking Points*, about their son's mental condition.

As further fallout from the verdict, federal and some state rules of evidence exclude or restrict testimony of an expert witness' conclusions on "ultimate" issues, including that of psychologist and psychiatrist expert witnesses on the issue of whether a criminal defendant is legally "insane." However, such is not the majority rule among the states today.

St. Elizabeths

Shortly after his trial, Hinckley wrote that the shooting was "the greatest love offering in the history of the world," and was upset that Foster did not reciprocate his love.

After being admitted, tests found that Hinckley was an "unpredictably dangerous" man who may harm himself, Jodie Foster or any other third party. In 1983 he told *Penthouse* that on a typical day he will

> "see a therapist, answer mail, play (his) guitar, listen to music, play pool, watch television, eat lousy food and take delicious medication."

He was allowed to leave the hospital for supervised visits with his parents in 1999, and longer unsupervised releases in 2000. These privileges were revoked when he was found to have smuggled materials about Foster back into the hospital. Hinckley was later allowed supervised visits in 2004 and 2005. Court hearings were held in September 2005 on whether he could have expanded privileges to leave the hospital. Some of the testimony during the hearings centered on whether Hinckley is capable of having a normal relationship with a woman and, if not, whether that would have any bearing on what danger he would pose to society.

On December 30, 2005, a federal judge ruled that Hinckley would be allowed visits, supervised by his parents, to their home in Williamsburg, Virginia. The judge ruled that Hinckley could have up to three visits of three nights and then four visits of four nights, each depending on the successful completion of the last. All of the experts who testified at Hinckley's 2005 conditional release hearing, including the government experts, agreed that his depression and psychotic disorder were in full remission and that he should have some expanded conditions of release.

After Hinckley requested further freedoms including two one-week visits with his parents, as well as a month-long visit, U.S. District Judge, Paul L. Friedman, denied that request on Wednesday, June 6, 2007; he did not deny the request out of a concern that Hinckley was not ready.

> The reasons the court has reached this decision rest with the hospital, not with Mr. Hinckley... the hospital has not taken the steps it must take before any such transition can begin.

On June 17, 2009, a Federal judge ruled that Hinckley would be given the ability to visit his mother for nine days at a time, rather than six, spend more time outside of the hospital, and even have a driver's license. This was done over the objections of the prosecutors who said that he was still a danger to others and had unhealthy and inappropriate thoughts about women. Records show that he has had sexual relations with two women, one who was married for a long time and another who has bipolar disorder. Hinckley recorded a song titled "Ballad of an Outlaw", which the prosecutors claim is "reflecting suicide and lawlessness."

See also

- United States federal laws governing offenders with mental diseases or defects

Further reading

- Clarke, James W. (1990). *On Being Mad or Merely Angry: John W. Hinckley, Jr., and Other Dangerous People*. Princeton University Press.
- Hinckley, John W. "The Insanity Defense and Me". *Newsweek*, September 20, 1982.

External links

- The Trial of John Hinckley, Jr., - University of Missouri at Kansas City Law School [1]
- The American Experience - John Hinckley, Jr. [2], by Julie Wolf.
- Crime Library - The John Hinckley Case [3] by Denise Noe.
- The Hinckley Double - underreported.com [4]
- The Day Hinckley Shot Reagan [5]
- Stalking Hinckley [6] by Eddie Dean, Washington City Paper, July 25-31, 1997.

Article Sources and Contributors

Assassination *Source*: http://en.wikipedia.org/?oldid=390423663 *Contributors*: 1 anonymous edits

History of assassination *Source*: http://en.wikipedia.org/?oldid=388072075 *Contributors*: Epeefleche

Richard Lawrence (failed assassin) *Source*: http://en.wikipedia.org/?oldid=385718366 *Contributors*: GenQuest

John Wilkes Booth *Source*: http://en.wikipedia.org/?oldid=389978766 *Contributors*: Kumioko

Charles J. Guiteau *Source*: http://en.wikipedia.org/?oldid=390010503 *Contributors*: Steven J. Anderson

Leon Czolgosz *Source*: http://en.wikipedia.org/?oldid=389037691 *Contributors*: Richard Arthur Norton (1958-)

Lee Harvey Oswald *Source*: http://en.wikipedia.org/?oldid=390392822 *Contributors*: Rodhullandemu

John F. Kennedy assassination conspiracy theories *Source*: http://en.wikipedia.org/?oldid=389941472 *Contributors*: Joegoodfriend

Sirhan Sirhan *Source*: http://en.wikipedia.org/?oldid=390600474 *Contributors*:

Assassination of Robert F. Kennedy *Source*: http://en.wikipedia.org/?oldid=386952245 *Contributors*: 1 anonymous edits

Lynette Fromme *Source*: http://en.wikipedia.org/?oldid=390684444 *Contributors*: WhisperToMe

Sara Jane Moore *Source*: http://en.wikipedia.org/?oldid=387692893 *Contributors*:

John Hinckley, Jr. *Source*: http://en.wikipedia.org/?oldid=390290713 *Contributors*: 1 anonymous edits

Image Sources, Licenses and Contributors

Image:Scale of justice 2.svg *Source*: http://bibliocm.bibliolabs.com/mwAnon/index.php?title=File:Scale_of_justice_2.svg *License*: Public Domain *Contributors*: User:DTR

Image:The Assassination of President Lincoln - Currier and Ives 2.png *Source*: http://bibliocm.bibliolabs.com/mwAnon/index.php?title=File:The_Assassination_of_President_Lincoln_-_Currier_and_Ives_2.png *License*: Public Domain *Contributors*: Currier & Ives, 1865.

Image:McKinleyAssassination.jpg *Source*: http://bibliocm.bibliolabs.com/mwAnon/index.php?title=File:McKinleyAssassination.jpg *License*: unknown *Contributors*: T. Dart Walker (1869-1914)

Image:JacksonAssassinationAttempt.jpg *Source*: http://bibliocm.bibliolabs.com/mwAnon/index.php?title=File:JacksonAssassinationAttempt.jpg *License*: Public Domain *Contributors*: Original uploader was Bonus Onus at en.wikipedia

File:John Wilkes Booth-portrait.jpg *Source*: http://bibliocm.bibliolabs.com/mwAnon/index.php?title=File:John_Wilkes_Booth-portrait.jpg *License*: Public Domain *Contributors*: Alex Gardner

File:John Wilkes Booth Signature2.svg *Source*: http://bibliocm.bibliolabs.com/mwAnon/index.php?title=File:John_Wilkes_Booth_Signature2.svg *License*: Public Domain *Contributors*: John Wilkes Booth

File:Tudor Hall.jpg *Source*: http://bibliocm.bibliolabs.com/mwAnon/index.php?title=File:Tudor_Hall.jpg *License*: Public Domain *Contributors*: User:JGHowes

File:Richmond Theatre (VA) in 1858.jpg *Source*: http://bibliocm.bibliolabs.com/mwAnon/index.php?title=File:Richmond_Theatre_(VA)_in_1858.jpg *License*: Public Domain *Contributors*: JGHowes

File:John Wilkes Booth playbill in Boston.jpg *Source*: http://bibliocm.bibliolabs.com/mwAnon/index.php?title=File:John_Wilkes_Booth_playbill_in_Boston.jpg *License*: Public Domain *Contributors*: User:JGHowes

File:Booths Caesar.jpg *Source*: http://bibliocm.bibliolabs.com/mwAnon/index.php?title=File:Booths_Caesar.jpg *License*: Public Domain *Contributors*: Unknown

File:Lucy Hale.jpg *Source*: http://bibliocm.bibliolabs.com/mwAnon/index.php?title=File:Lucy_Hale.jpg *License*: Public Domain *Contributors*: User:JGHowes

File:Soldiers-Home-Lincoln-Cottage.jpg *Source*: http://bibliocm.bibliolabs.com/mwAnon/index.php?title=File:Soldiers-Home-Lincoln-Cottage.jpg *License*: Public Domain *Contributors*: w:Jack E. BoucherJack E. Boucher

File:John Wilkes Booth playbill.jpg *Source*: http://bibliocm.bibliolabs.com/mwAnon/index.php?title=File:John_Wilkes_Booth_playbill.jpg *License*: Public Domain *Contributors*: Ford's Theatre

File:The Assassination of President Lincoln - Currier and Ives 2.png *Source*: http://bibliocm.bibliolabs.com/mwAnon/index.php?title=File:The_Assassination_of_President_Lincoln_-_Currier_and_Ives_2.png *License*: Public Domain *Contributors*: Currier & Ives, 1865.

File:Booth escape route.svg *Source*: http://bibliocm.bibliolabs.com/mwAnon/index.php?title=File:Booth_escape_route.svg *License*: Public Domain *Contributors*: User:Kuara

File:John Wilkes Booth wanted poster.jpg *Source*: http://bibliocm.bibliolabs.com/mwAnon/index.php?title=File:John_Wilkes_Booth_wanted_poster.jpg *License*: Public Domain *Contributors*: Dantadd, Davepape, Frank C. Müller, Man vyi, Mogelzahn, PaterMcFly

File:Garrett Farm.gif *Source*: http://bibliocm.bibliolabs.com/mwAnon/index.php?title=File:Garrett_Farm.gif *License*: Public Domain *Contributors*: Unknown, owned by NPS as stated here

File:Jwb farm.jpg *Source*: http://bibliocm.bibliolabs.com/mwAnon/index.php?title=File:Jwb_farm.jpg *License*: GNU Free Documentation License *Contributors*: User:JGHowes

File:Booth family gravesite.jpg *Source*: http://bibliocm.bibliolabs.com/mwAnon/index.php?title=File:Booth_family_gravesite.jpg *License*: Attribution *Contributors*: User:JGHowes

File:Charles J Guiteau.jpg *Source*: http://bibliocm.bibliolabs.com/mwAnon/index.php?title=File:Charles_J_Guiteau.jpg *License*: Public Domain *Contributors*: User:Connormah

File:Charles Guiteau Signature.svg *Source*: http://bibliocm.bibliolabs.com/mwAnon/index.php?title=File:Charles_Guiteau_Signature.svg *License*: Public Domain *Contributors*: User:Connormah

Image:Garfield assassination engraving cropped.jpg *Source*: http://bibliocm.bibliolabs.com/mwAnon/index.php?title=File:Garfield_assassination_engraving_cropped.jpg *License*: Public Domain *Contributors*: A. Berghaus and C. Upham, published in Frank Leslie's Illustrated Newspaper.

Image:Guiteau's pistol.jpg *Source*: http://bibliocm.bibliolabs.com/mwAnon/index.php?title=File:Guiteau's_pistol.jpg *License*: Public Domain *Contributors*: James Dabney McCabe

File:Guiteau cartoon2.jpg *Source*: http://bibliocm.bibliolabs.com/mwAnon/index.php?title=File:Guiteau_cartoon2.jpg *License*: Public Domain *Contributors*: Published by Keppler & Schwarzmann, signed by James Albert Wales with his reversed initials

File:Czol photo 1900 - found in effects.jpg *Source*: http://bibliocm.bibliolabs.com/mwAnon/index.php?title=File:Czol_photo_1900_-_found_in_effects.jpg *License*: Public Domain *Contributors*: unknown photographer about 1900

File:Leon Czolgosz Signature.svg *Source*: http://bibliocm.bibliolabs.com/mwAnon/index.php?title=File:Leon_Czolgosz_Signature.svg *License*: Public Domain *Contributors*: User:Connormah

File:Anarchy-symbol.svg *Source*: http://bibliocm.bibliolabs.com/mwAnon/index.php?title=File:Anarchy-symbol.svg *License*: Public Domain *Contributors*: User:Arcy, User:Froztbyte, User:Linuxerist

File:BlackFlagSymbol.svg *Source*: http://bibliocm.bibliolabs.com/mwAnon/index.php?title=File:BlackFlagSymbol.svg *License*: Creative Commons Attribution 3.0 *Contributors*: Original uploader was Jsymmetry at en.wikipedia

Image:McKinley Monument.jpg *Source*: http://bibliocm.bibliolabs.com/mwAnon/index.php?title=File:McKinley_Monument.jpg *License*: Attribution *Contributors*: User:Sherurcij

Image:First photograph of Leon F. Czolgosz, the assassin of President William McKinley, in jail.jpg *Source*: http://bibliocm.bibliolabs.com/mwAnon/index.php?title=File:First_photograph_of_Leon_F._Czolgosz,_the_assassin_of_President_William_McKinley,_in_jail.jpg *License*: Public Domain *Contributors*: Judge Company

Image Sources, Licenses and Contributors

Image:Czol following day.jpg *Source*: http://bibliocm.bibliolabs.com/mwAnon/index.php?title=File:Czol_following_day.jpg *License*: Public Domain *Contributors*: unidentified police photographer

Image:Czol execution card.jpg *Source*: http://bibliocm.bibliolabs.com/mwAnon/index.php?title=File:Czol_execution_card.jpg *License*: Public Domain *Contributors*: Berean Hunter, Infrogmation, Sherurcij

Image:Paul Father Czol.jpg *Source*: http://bibliocm.bibliolabs.com/mwAnon/index.php?title=File:Paul_Father_Czol.jpg *License*: Public Domain *Contributors*: Uncredited; looks like police mugshot

Image:Jacob Czol.jpg *Source*: http://bibliocm.bibliolabs.com/mwAnon/index.php?title=File:Jacob_Czol.jpg *License*: Public Domain *Contributors*: uncredited, probably police mugshot photographer

File:CE2892.jpg *Source*: http://bibliocm.bibliolabs.com/mwAnon/index.php?title=File:CE2892.jpg *License*: unknown *Contributors*: Bradipus, Docu, Frank C. Müller, Infrogmation, LobStoR, Lokal Profil, Marku1988, Nard the Bard

File:Lee Harvey Oswald Signature.svg *Source*: http://bibliocm.bibliolabs.com/mwAnon/index.php?title=File:Lee_Harvey_Oswald_Signature.svg *License*: Public Domain *Contributors*: User:Connormah

File:CE2595.jpg *Source*: http://bibliocm.bibliolabs.com/mwAnon/index.php?title=File:CE2595.jpg *License*: Public Domain *Contributors*: Bradipus, Docu, Evrik, Frank C. Müller, High Contrast, Infrogmation, Jmabel, LobStoR, TommyBee

File:4911MagazineNOLA.JPG *Source*: http://bibliocm.bibliolabs.com/mwAnon/index.php?title=File:4911MagazineNOLA.JPG *License*: Creative Commons Attribution-Sharealike 3.0 *Contributors*: Infrogmation of New Orleans

File:Pizzo Exh B-Oswald leaflets FPFC-WH Vol21 139.jpg *Source*: http://bibliocm.bibliolabs.com/mwAnon/index.php?title=File:Pizzo_Exh_B-Oswald_leaflets_FPFC-WH_Vol21_139.jpg *License*: unknown *Contributors*: Bradipus, Docu, Infrogmation, LobStoR, Nard the Bard

File:TexasTheater oswaldsSeat.jpg *Source*: http://bibliocm.bibliolabs.com/mwAnon/index.php?title=File:TexasTheater_oswaldsSeat.jpg *License*: Creative Commons Attribution-Sharealike 2.5 *Contributors*: Nathan Beach

File:GeraldHill-B.jpg *Source*: http://bibliocm.bibliolabs.com/mwAnon/index.php?title=File:GeraldHill-B.jpg *License*: Public Domain *Contributors*: Bradipus, Gothic2, Infrogmation

Image:CE795.jpg *Source*: http://bibliocm.bibliolabs.com/mwAnon/index.php?title=File:CE795.jpg *License*: Public Domain *Contributors*: Bradipus, Estillbham, Juiced lemon, LobStoR, Mattes

File:Lho-133A.jpg *Source*: http://bibliocm.bibliolabs.com/mwAnon/index.php?title=File:Lho-133A.jpg *License*: unknown *Contributors*: Bradipus, Docu, Infrogmation, LobStoR, Nard the Bard

File:Oswaldrifle.jpg *Source*: http://bibliocm.bibliolabs.com/mwAnon/index.php?title=File:Oswaldrifle.jpg *License*: Public Domain *Contributors*: Bradipus, Nemo5576, Oxam Hartog, Shizhao, Tomia, 2 anonymous edits

Image:John F. Kennedy motorcade, Dallas crop.png *Source*: http://bibliocm.bibliolabs.com/mwAnon/index.php?title=File:John_F._Kennedy_motorcade,_Dallas_crop.png *License*: Public Domain *Contributors*: Victor Hugo King, who placed the photograph in the public domain (presumably when he gave it to the Library of Congress).

Image:wanted for treason.jpg *Source*: http://bibliocm.bibliolabs.com/mwAnon/index.php?title=File:Wanted_for_treason.jpg *License*: unknown *Contributors*: Anon

Image:Dealey Plaza 2003.jpg *Source*: http://bibliocm.bibliolabs.com/mwAnon/index.php?title=File:Dealey_Plaza_2003.jpg *License*: Public Domain *Contributors*: Brodie319

Image:JFK Wooden Fence.jpg *Source*: http://bibliocm.bibliolabs.com/mwAnon/index.php?title=File:JFK_Wooden_Fence.jpg *License*: Creative Commons Attribution-Sharealike 2.5 *Contributors*: User:BenFrantzDale

File:Robert F Kennedy crop.jpg *Source*: http://bibliocm.bibliolabs.com/mwAnon/index.php?title=File:Robert_F_Kennedy_crop.jpg *License*: Public Domain *Contributors*: User:elcobbola

Image:Robert Kennedy grave.jpg *Source*: http://bibliocm.bibliolabs.com/mwAnon/index.php?title=File:Robert_Kennedy_grave.jpg *License*: Creative Commons Attribution 2.0 *Contributors*: howieluvzus

Image:AV89-26-14 600d.jpg *Source*: http://bibliocm.bibliolabs.com/mwAnon/index.php?title=File:AV89-26-14_600d.jpg *License*: Public Domain *Contributors*: BrokenSphere, Erik Baas, Fanra, Infrogmation, Rfsjim, Sylfred1977

Image:Reagan assassination attempt 3.jpg *Source*: http://bibliocm.bibliolabs.com/mwAnon/index.php?title=File:Reagan_assassination_attempt_3.jpg *License*: Public Domain *Contributors*: Frank C. Müller, Happyme22, Man vyi, 2 anonymous edits

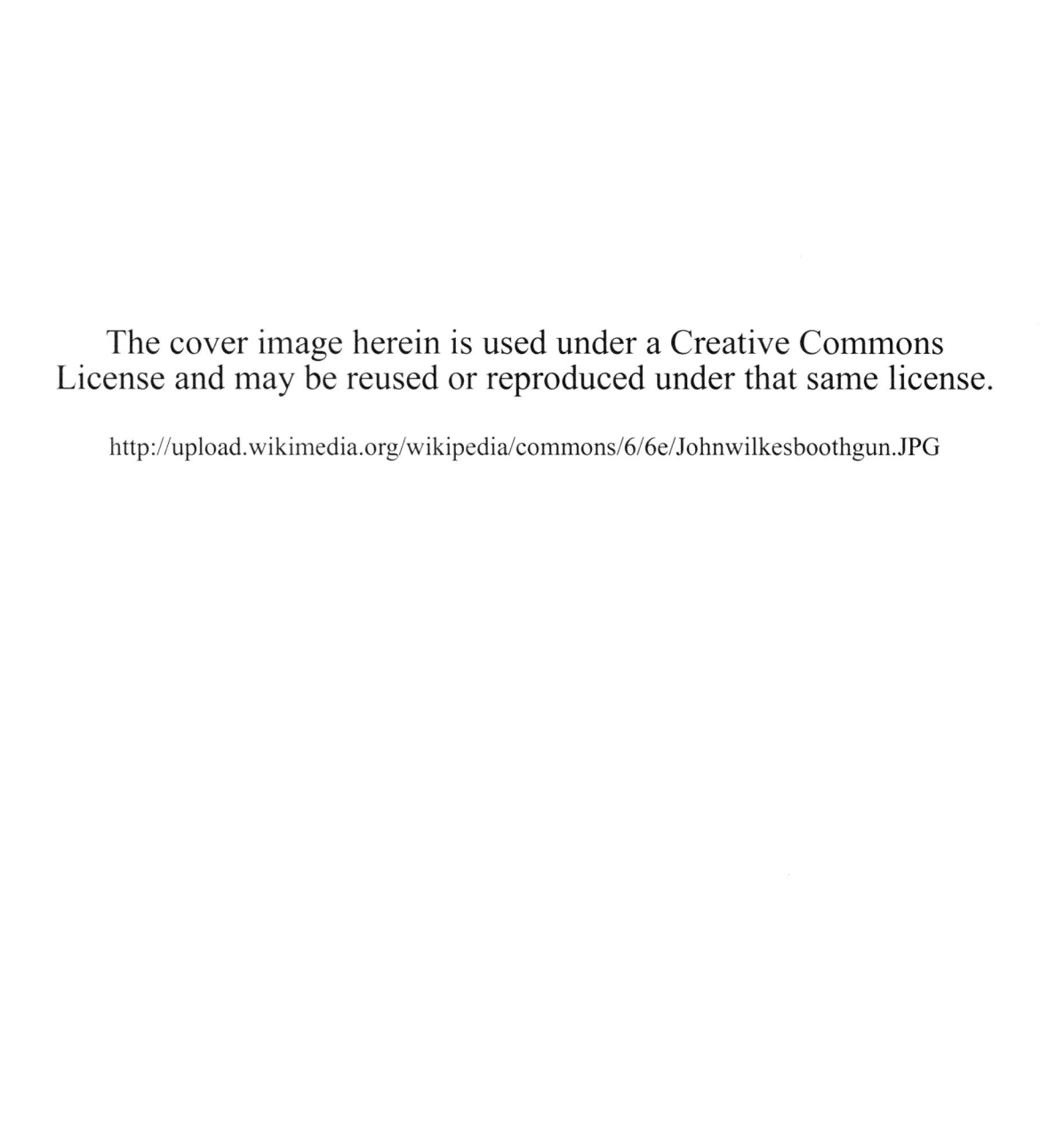

The cover image herein is used under a Creative Commons License and may be reused or reproduced under that same license.

http://upload.wikimedia.org/wikipedia/commons/6/6e/Johnwilkesboothgun.JPG

CPSIA information can be obtained at www.ICGtesting.com
Printed in the USA
267508BV00003B/5/P